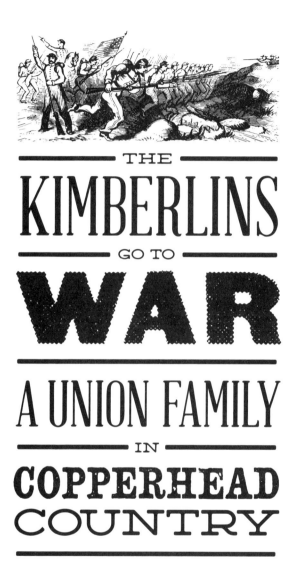

THE
KIMBERLINS
GO TO
WAR
A UNION FAMILY
IN
COPPERHEAD
COUNTRY

MICHAEL B. MURPHY

INDIANA HISTORICAL SOCIETY PRESS | 2016

© 2016 Indiana Historical Society Press

This book is a publication of the
Indiana Historical Society Press

Eugene and Marilyn Glick Indiana History Center
450 West Ohio Street
Indianapolis, Indiana 45202-3269 USA
www.indianahistory.org

Telephone orders 1-800-447-1830

Fax orders 1-317-234-0562

Online orders @ http://shop.indianahistory.org

Names: Murphy, Michael B., 1957- author.
Title: The Kimberlins go to war : a Union family in copperhead country /
  Michael B. Murphy.
Description: Indianapolis, Indiana : Indiana Historical Society Press, 2016.
  | Includes bibliographical references and index.
Identifiers: LCCN 2016001244 (print) | LCCN 2016020897 (ebook) | ISBN
  9780871953773 (cloth : alk. paper) | ISBN 9780871953780 (epub)
Subjects: LCSH: Scott County (Ind.)–History, Military–19th century. |
  Kimberlin family. | Indiana–History–Civil War, 1861-1865. | United
  States–History–Civil War, 1861-1865–Biography. |
  Soldiers–Indiana–Scott County–Biography. | Scott County
  (Ind.)–Biography.
Classification: LCC F532.S35 M87 2016 (print) | LCC F532.S35 (ebook) | DDC
  977.2/183–dc23
LC record available at https://lccn.loc.gov/2016001244

The paper in this publication meets the minimum requirements of American National
Standard for Information Sciences—Permanence of Paper for Printed Library Materials,
ANSI Z39. 48–1984

The Kimberlins Go to War: A Union Family in Copperhead Country was made possible through the generous support of the Ian and Mimi Rolland Foundation and the Herbert Simon Family Foundation.

This book is dedicated to Thelma Gilbert Hogue, who is descended through the Kimberlin line from "old" Abraham Kimberlin, through James Washington Kimberlin, John Kimberlin, and Sarah Irene Kimberlin. It was Thelma who had the foresight to preserve the invaluable cache of Kimberlin letters that date from the late 1700s, who graciously granted me access to these letters, and who sat by my side for hours reading the handwriting of her ancestors so that I could transcribe and understand. This book, in fact the ability to bring the Kimberlin history alive, would have been impossible without her wisdom.

I also dedicate this work to my father, James E. Murphy, who taught me to love writing, and to my mother, Barbara Lill Murphy, who taught me to relish family history and to persevere.

Contents

Acknowledgments

I would like to acknowledge the original genealogical work of Denise Thompson Moody, a Kimberlin descendant who first brought their story to me. Denise intrigued me with the results of her work, especially the tales of Kimberlins who served in the Civil War. Denise told me about the existence of the Kimberlin letters and encouraged me to write about the family.

The reference desk staff of the Indiana State Library, the Indiana Historical Society William Henry Smith Memorial Library, the Scott County Historical Society, and the National Archives provided patient service to me as I sought to make sense of their massive resources. Alan F. January of the Indiana State Archives was particularly helpful in teaching me how to begin my archival research.

Three Indiana University–Purdue University at Indianapolis professors—Doctors Jack McGivigan, Robert Barrows, and Kevin Robbins—reviewed many drafts and suggested revisions. Terry Winschel, former chief historian of the Vicksburg National Military Park, went out his way to help me understand the entire Vicksburg campaign. Cathy Parise brought an eye for detail to proper formatting.

I am also grateful to Herb Simon and Ian Rolland for their patronage, and to my editors at the Indiana Historical Society Press, Ray E. Boomhower and Kathy Breen. They saw a story worth sharing.

Finally, I would like to thank my sons, Brendan and Kevin, and family and friends who have put up with me, and given me encouraging words and gentle prods over time. They are too numerous to name, but they know who they are. I am a very lucky man.

1

War Comes to Indiana

As July 7, 1861, dawned, talk of war was in the air in Lexington, Indiana. The county seat of Scott County was abuzz with the latest news about the Southern rebellion. The *Madison Daily and Evening Courier* told of skirmishes between Federal troops and "secesh" forces at Harpers Ferry and Falling Waters, Virginia. Closer to home, word had come that William A. Sanderson had organized a new regiment, the Twenty-third Indiana Volunteers, on June 24, and was recruiting across the second congressional district.[1] A Captain Ferguson had been in town looking for strong young men. All takers were to meet him in Charlestown by sunset on July 8.

Jacob T. Kimberlin was a twenty-one-year-old farmhand, the eighth of ten children of Jacob J. and Elizabeth Kimberlin, of nearby Nabb. Unlike most families in the area, all of the Kimberlin children had survived early childhood. In the mid-1800s, one-half of all Hoosier children died before the age of four from such common causes as diphtheria in the winter and dysentery in the summer.[2] The Kimberlin sons worked on the farm, or as coopers in town, while the three girls shared the household chores. Their mother had died in 1844.

We do not know Jacob T.'s thoughts as he decided to sign up for three years of military service, but if there is comfort in numbers, he had plenty of it. Jacob walked out of Lexington on the Charlestown road on July 8 with his older brother, John J., and his cousins, William H. H. Kimberlin, Benjamin F. Kimberlin, and James Stark.[3] These five young men could not have known at the time that none of them would ever return home. They simply knew that the Kimberlins were going to war.

This is the story of the Kimberlin family that sent thirty-three fathers and sons, brothers and cousins, to fight for the Union cause during the

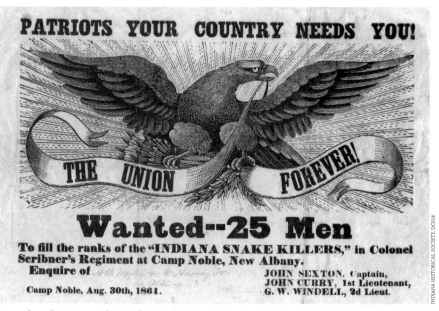

Posted at the start of the Civil War, this broadside urged young men to volunteer for military service at Camp Noble in New Albany, Indiana, for a regiment to be known as the "Indiana Snake Killers."

Civil War. Ten family members were killed, wounded, or died of battlefield disease—a 30 percent casualty rate that is unmatched in recorded Scott County history. Of the 135 known deaths of Scott County soldiers,[4] ten were members of the Kimberlin clan.[5]

While we know that the Kimberlins suffered disproportionately, our only clues to their feelings about the war come from forty letters to and from the battlefield that have survived. Were they fighting to save the Union or to free the slaves? How did they express grief over the loss of a brother? Did they keep up with their business and the women at home? And what did they think about "secesh" neighbors in southern Indiana who tried to undermine the Union cause? The answers to these questions will help determine if the Kimberlins were unusual in their patriotism or simply acting as any Union family would in an area of the nation that came to be known as Copperhead Country.

A Military Tradition

The Kimberlins were not new to adversity or to war. Their German-born patriarch, John Jacob Peter Kimberlin, and his wife, Sarah

Clendenin, raised five boys on a small farm in Hampshire County, Virginia, in the mid-1700s. When hostilities between England and the American colonies broke out, the patriarch's son, also named John, was commissioned a second lieutenant in the Bedford County, Pennsylvania, Second Battalion, by Assembly Speaker John Morton.[6] Following the Revolutionary War, John and his wife, Ruth Jones, settled in Greene County, Pennsylvania, where they were neighbors with Thomas Hughes, another veteran.

Hughes and Kimberlin must have discussed opportunities in western Virginia (now Kentucky and Indiana). When the Clark's Grant Board of Commissioners partitioned the 135,000-acre federal grant to officers who had served under George Rogers Clark, it awarded Captain William Harrod, founder of Louisville and brother of the founder of Harrodsburg, 3,000 acres.[7] Hughes and Kimberlin cooperated in a deal whereby Hughes purchased Lot Number 264 from Harrod, and then resold the 500-acre plot to Kimberlin on April 16, 1804, for $1,600.[8] In April 1805, just days after the Treaty of Grouseland opened up the land from the Ohio River to Rockford (north of Seymour),[9] Kimberlin brought his sons, Daniel and Isaac, by flatboat from Redstone, Pennsylvania, near the present-day site of Madison, where they walked to Lot 264, one-quarter of a mile northwest of the present town of Nabb.[10] There they built a white-oak cabin, which stood until 1876, on what is now known as Kimberlin Creek, and became the first white settlers of the area that fifteen years later became Scott County.[11] Over the next four years, the other eight Kimberlin children and their mother came in small groups to fill their home on the frontier. They would make history again in 1812.

Pigeon Roost

Five miles west of the Kimberlin homestead, the Collings family from Nelson County, Kentucky, settled in 1809 at the juncture of the Three Notch Trail (now US 31) and the Cincinnati Trace. The trail was a well-used Indian path that connected the Falls of the Ohio River with the point where Fall Creek empties into the White River. The trace was a commercial road cut by Ephraim Kibbey from Cincinnati to Vincennes between 1799 and 1805.[12] The settlement became known as Pigeon Roost.

In the late summer of 1812, while the able-bodied men of Pigeon Roost were fighting with American troops near Detroit, Shawnee and Pottawatomi Indians were told of a British bounty of five dollars per American scalp. On September 3, Indians attacked the Pigeon Roost settlement and butchered twenty-two residents, including a baby torn from the womb of Rachel Collings. The bodies were scalped, cut in strips, and hung from nearby trees. Some of the survivors ran to the Kimberlin cabin for protection.[13]

Within three days, 596 volunteers from Captain John Blizzard's company of Kentucky Volunteers (including Isaac Kimberlin and John Williams) camped on the Kimberlin farm, preparing to search for the marauders.[14] The cabin was ordered reinforced as a blockhouse and patrols were sent as far north as the Kankakee River, but no one was ever punished for what came to be called the Pigeon Roost Massacre.[15] Nevertheless, John Kimberlin's farm was trampled by the Kentucky troops, and the family's livestock and grain were taken.

Twenty years later, the eighty-one year old Kimberlin, now blind, and his wife, Ruth, petitioned Congress for reimbursement with the help of their son, Daniel, himself a veteran of the Battle of Tippecanoe as a rifleman in Captain James Bigger's Rifle Company.[16] The petition read in part: "for three days during which time the corps above named pulled down my fences, out and carried off my corn, using it as forage for their horses, took many articles of provisions for the use of said volunteers while at said encampment. The value of articles thus taken is estimated to exceed one hundred dollars, for which no compensation has been given."[17] During the first session of the Twenty-Third Congress, U.S. Senator John Tipton of Indiana introduced Senate Bill 38, which the Committee on Claims approved on December 31, 1833. John Kimberlin was paid $150 on May 26, 1834, ten months before his death.[18]

As settlers flowed into Scott County, mainly from Kentucky, the Kimberlins intermarried with other settler families: the Whitlachs, Houghs, Starkes, and Williams. They lived on homesteads in the Nabb area, within a short walk from one another. They recorded several firsts—the first marriage in Scott County (Daniel Kimberlin to Ursula Brinton, May 7, 1812);[19] the founding of the first Baptist church (by Sarah Whitlach Gladden in 1819);[20] and one of the first schools (the Kimberlin School, located three miles west of Lexington on the Vienna road).[21] The Kimberlins were also an integral part of the transformation of the Scott County economy from subsistence to a commercially based system.

General Jefferson C. Davis (left) in his tent with one of his officers. A veteran of the Mexican-American War, Davis later mortally wounded a fellow Union army general, William "Bull" Nelson.

Mustering In

When the four Kimberlin men reached Camp Noble, on the site of today's Floyd County Fairgrounds, for mustering in on July 27, 1861, they were treated to the sight of Indiana's first military hero of the Civil War, Jefferson C. Davis, second in command at Fort Sumter when Confederate troops shelled the island fort into submission in April 1861.[22] After the fort's surrender, the Clark County native was sent back to Indiana to serve as a mustering officer and to rally support for the war.[23]

For the Kimberlins, Camp Noble was where they met and made new friends such as James Royse and John Hardin, both from neighboring Washington County. It was also where they were divided into companies and received their military equipment. The Kimberlins stuck together in Company I. Royse joined Company C and Hardin was assigned to Company E.[24] In a letter to his father, Hardin described Camp Noble as "crowded with about one-thousand soldiers in camp."[25] Hardin listed his supplies, with some editorial comment:

> 1.Bread, and plenty of it. 2. Bacon, some to sell. 3. Beef, some of its spoils. 4. Coffee, some to sell. 5. Rice, plenty. 6. Shugar, not so plenty. 7. Molasses, not so plenty. 8. Potatoes, plenty of them. 9. Dried apples, plenty. 10. Blackberries, sell bread for these. 11. Onions. 12. Pepper. 13. Salt.
> Also, Tin cups, pans, knives and forks to eat out of.[26]

The Royse and Hardin letters complement the Kimberlin writings, and together they weave a common experience through individual recollections of boredom, constant marching, letters from home, intense battles, and more letters to sisters, girlfriends, cousins, and parents. As the Twenty-Third Indiana left for Saint Louis on August 17, 1861, it was the state's second regiment to go off to war unarmed. The guns did not catch up to the regiment until it arrived at Camp General Smith in Paducah, Kentucky.[27] John J. Kimberlin wrote to his cousin, Jacob R. Kimberlin, about the camp setup:

> Jake, I would not come home if I could get a honorable discharge for the best two horsed in our Reg. Tell Milla that I found the regulations of the army altogether different from her predictions and if she has got a son in the service she may rest assured that he will get plenty to eat and to wear and his treatment otherways will depend upon his behavior. . . . I will tell you we are fixed just so that it will take arite smart little army to take us. We now about 9 thousand as near as I can find out and just as good as can be. . . . Our artillery consist of two sixty-four pounders and other peces too numerous to mention Jake if you was to see our flying artillery it would make your white eyes role worse than they ever did before Jake we have got all of our equipment and it is thought that we will move before many days.[28]

Paducah became home to the Kimberlins for more than six months. For the most part, it was six months of inaction, interspersed by orders to battle, then disappointment at missing the "fun." In a November 10, 1861, joint letter to their brother, Jacob R., William, and Benjamin talk of weariness from marching, and send thanks for goodies:

> We have been on a march three days. There was a battle at Collumbus on the 7th. We were first ordered to a little town called Mayfield, but before we got there we were ordered to Collumbus, but before we got

there we heard the battle was over and we turned back to Paducah . . . tell our sisters [Polly Ann, Betsy, and Maria] that sent them cakes to us by Mr. Sullivan that they come to us in good order, we also recived some apples from Father and two pair of socks apiece and one pair for Jacob [T.] Kimberlin . . . you can tell the girls and Father that they was all very thankfully recived although we was not particularly in need for Uncle Sam has provided well for us so far . . . more than I expected when I volunteered.[29]

Cousin James Stark, also of the Twenty-Third, viewed winter camp at Paducah as a chance to rest and reflect on two overriding subjects of camp talk—women and "the cause." In a letter to his cousin, Jacob R., who had stayed home to take care of the family farm, Stark talks of preparing to see "the elephant" (the Rebel army):

We have built a good sized fort. . . . we have several guns mounted but only two 64 pounders the rest is 32 artil. 432 cavalry landed this week . . . Jake I must tell you I haven't spoke to a purty women since I left Indiana and I am almost froze to see some of the old Scott and Clark girls. Jake tell them my love is with them, if I live. Jake true love is sweet but love of country is sweeter . . . if I could sacrifice the last drop of my blood if it would put a end to the rebellion. I may lose it anyhow but I cannot spill my blood in a better cause.[30]

A print depicts Confederate soldiers firing cannons from an artillery battery, bombarding Fort Sumter, the federal sea fort in Charleston, South Carolina.

Civilian onlookers and Union teamsters panic as the Confederates take control of the field during the Battle of Bull Run, July 21, 1861, near Manassas, Virginia.

And on Christmas Day, 1861, Stark expressed his thoughts about women, embellished, as they were, by alcohol:

> We have a fine Christmas hair. I am taking mine on guard. Our capton gave us a treat this morning. I wish that I was up thair today to make a set to some of them good looking girls for I have not seen any good looking one since I left home. I will be back some of these days and then I am coming to see them. Well you must excuse my nonsense and bad wrighting as I drank a little too much this morning. Wright and let me no how you get a long with all of the girls.[31]

Secesh

While the Kimberlin men were settling into camp routine in Paducah, emotions were stirring back home in Scott County. The initial reaction to the fall of Fort Sumter was a burst of patriotism, as expressed by Lexington, Indiana, teenager Sarah Waldschmidt Young Bovard in her personal diary: "Fort Sumter was taken today by the rebels or devils—the latter sounds the best. Everyone talks of War. Indiana begins to wake up."[32] Even the Democratic *Indianapolis Sentinel* initially backed the Union effort and Republican Indiana governor Oliver Morton proclaimed, "There is now no choice in the matter. The Government must be sustained."[33] But as news of the disaster at what came to be known as the First Battle of Bull Run zipped across the telegraph lines, the reality of what had occurred near that little town of Manassas, Virginia, began to settle in. Husbands and wives, families, and even entire towns debated the wisdom of taking up arms against the South. Most of the people of southern Indiana had "connections" in Kentucky and Virginia going back several generations. Cousins would be fighting cousins, and in some cases, brother would be fighting brother. In a letter from J. B. Otey to John G. Davis, Otey said, "I cannot take sides against the South. The bones of my ancestors lie mouldering there. My connections are there. Everything dear to me in the way of kindred is there, and I must and will be there."[34]

Those Northerners who sympathized with the South quickly became known as "secesh" (short for secessionists). It became one of the most divisive labels that could be pinned on a Hoosier, as Sarah's diary recounts: "Catherine and Ethe come awhile, then go to Mother's. They all look at me as they would a thief because I am not a secesh."[35] The debate even encroached on church life: "Mother comes by going to meeting. Stops long enough to wish old Lincoln dead."[36] It also disrupted the local schoolyard: "A fight takes place at the schoolhouse. Three secesh and one Union man, of course."[37] The young chronicler of Lexington life rarely allowed a diary entry to pass without mentioning some incident or debate involving the war: "Yesterday was a day to be remembered. We went to Gilead [local church] to the soldiers meeting but the secesh feeling was too much for us."[38]

Copperhead Country

During the latter half of 1861, two new names were given those who questioned the Union war effort: Copperhead and Butternut. Copperhead referred to the poisonous snake whose habitat included most of the South, and Butternut referred to the color of uniform that some Confederate troops wore. The names were used interchangeably but their definition, even today, escapes precision. Indiana historian Emma Lou Thornbrough captured the basic equation. According to her, "If one accepts a recent definition of Copperheadism as avid opposition to the [Abraham]

Lincoln administration, and adds to it avid opposition to Governor Morton, the number of Copperheads in Indiana was large. Those who wanted to see the Union permanently divided and who were ready actively to help the Confederate cause were very few."[39] The Copperhead movement may have begun to smolder with the reluctance on the part of southern Hoosiers to fight their "connections" but it was given oxygen and fanned to a roaring fire by fear and economic hardship.

In 1850 one-half of all Hoosiers were not native to the state, and 39 percent (162,000) of these came from slave states.[40] The bulk of Indiana's immigrant residents were of German or Irish ancestry, and they naturally feared the competition that could come from the arrival of free black labor. The German language newspapers *Indiana Volksblatt* (Indianapolis) and *Staats Zeitwag* (Fort Wayne) even made appeals *for* bigotry.[41] In 1851 Hoosiers overwhelmingly ratified the infamous Article 13 of the new Indiana Constitution that banned the immigration of "Negroes" into the state. This earned the state the moniker of "most conservative Midwestern state" in its treatment of African Americans.[42]

The attitude toward African Americans certainly was unsympathetic even thirteen years later. In a letter home from the Twenty-Third, regimental clerk Alt Perring wrote to a Mrs. Alderice: "In regard to contrabands on your farm, I do not know whether you are joking or serious, but I hope you will not establish a colony of African descent anywhere upon your premises."[43] During the 1861 legislative session, the Indiana General Assembly passed a resolution clarifying that the state's resources should not be used to destroy slavery or the rights of the states.[44] This sentiment toward African Americans is not surprising in the context of the times because southern Indiana was part of the Ohio River Valley economy. Prior to the railroads coming to the state in the 1840s, the bulk of the region's goods were shipped across the Ohio River to the Southern states. Southern Indiana was for all purposes, a "southern economy."

2

Scott County Looks South to Trade

When John Kimberlin and his sons, Daniel and Isaac, arrived at their new homestead in Clark's Grant in April 1805, they were completing a trek that had been made thousands of times in previous years by their friends and neighbors who had migrated from Virginia, North Carolina, and Kentucky. The Cumberland Gap and the Ohio River provided natural outlets for the dream of making a better life in the land west of the Appalachian Mountains. With the founding of Harrodsburg and Louisville, Kentucky, families had economic centers on which they could focus their migration plans, as well as protective stockades where they could go for safe harbor and to trade. Almost immediately after the end of the Revolutionary War, restless residents of the Tidewater made the trans-Appalachian trip, setting up an economy that would be based on the knowledge, tools, and habits of their native lands.

Subsistence Economy

The Kimberlins were the first whites to face the land of scattered timber and fields and meadows interspersed with small creeks and gently rolling hills that became Scott County. The tools they had at their disposal were the same that had been available to earlier settlers of Kentucky—an axe, a long-barreled rifle, a sickle, a hoe, a brush harrow, and a wooden mold board plow were the basics to create a livable, survivable space in the wilderness. If a settler was particularly fortunate he might have a team of oxen.[1] The Kimberlins most likely had a mule.

Soil science had not yet advanced to anything close to modern standards. Today we know what the Kimberlins could not have known, that in their vicinity were four distinct soil types, classified today as Scottsburg Silt Loam, Dekalb Silt Loam, Waverly Silt Loam, and Volusia Silt Loam.[2] Each had its own characteristics, and each was amenable to particular crops.

The Kimberlins built their white-oak cabin near a spring, on a gentle rise above the banks of what is now called Kimberlin Creek. The land fell gently away to the north and west, with the tree line of the creek visible about 200 yards away. To the east was a dense bog from which flowed two substantial springs with enough water to support a rudimentary mill and, maybe someday, a tannery. Since their arrival coincided with planting season, they would have immediately set about felling trees, with the stumps left standing, and then would have broken up the soil among the stumps and scattered corn or wheat seed by hand among the freshly turned soil.

The Kimberlins and their fellow pioneers did not engage in commerce as we think of it today. They were primarily subsistence farmers, killing or harvesting what they ate and making by hand anything they needed for comfort. Their diet would have consisted of salt pork, potatoes, and dried fruits and vegetables, including peaches, apples, pumpkins, beans, and corn. Because of the way they cooked their food, simmering over an open fire for hours, most vitamins and much of the nutritional value was cooked out of the food before it was consumed.[3] There certainly was a crude system of bartering among homesteads, but there was no commercial trade in those first years. Even if a surplus was produced, markets were distant, and there were no roads. The nearest town, Madison, on the Ohio River seventeen miles away, was not founded until 1808.

We do not know how many fellow settlers the Kimberlins had to commiserate with as they tried to establish civilization in the land between the Muscatatuck and Ohio Rivers. The 1800 federal census for Knox County in the Northwest Territory, of which the Kimberlin homestead was a part, is lost.[4] We do know that historians estimate one-half of the population in the newly established Indiana Territory in 1800 lived in Clark's Grant or along the Wabash River near Vincennes.[5] County data for all counties in the 1810 Federal Census are also lost,[6] but the "Report on Arts and Manufactures of the Territory of Indiana" published that year shows only limited commerce with a lower total value of manufactured goods ($196,532) than any other territory or state except the Illinois, Michigan, and Louisiana Territories.[7] This does not mean we cannot draw some broad inferences from the data as long as we do not try to reach conclusions on the Kimberlins' little corner of the world.

The 1810 census divided the Indiana Territory into six reporting divisions. Only the fourth division, not specified as to location, reported much detail. In this division, Assistant Marshal Joseph Brown documented one wheat mill, three horse mills, ten gristmills, and six sawmills. These were the primary engines for running the pioneer subsistence economy. True manufacturing was limited to one nailery, three gunpowder mills, and thirteen distilleries whose product was mostly for home consumption. The data available clearly show that the Kimberlins were not alone in facing tough conditions for survival. They were pioneers in the economic sense of the term as they gathered their sustenance from the fields and raw materials they had nearby, consuming almost all their work product themselves.

After the War of 1812, in which Daniel Kimberlin served at the Battle of Tippecanoe, migration to the Indiana Territory exploded. By 1815 the territory had an estimated 64,000 inhabitants, nearly triple the 24,000 in 1810,[8] and civilization began to take a more traditional form in the vicinity of the Kimberlin homestead. In June 1813 William McFarland established the first trading post and tavern at the future site of the town of Lexington. The spot chosen for the town was along the Cincinnati Trace where it intersected with an Indian trail that led to the Ohio River. The site was protected from the south and west by low hills, creating a small watershed.[9] The first post office, with James Ward as postmaster, was established in Lexington in 1814 and the second newspaper in the Indiana Territory, the *Western Eagle*, moved from Madison and began publishing in Lexington in July 1815.[10] The only surviving copies of the *Western Eagle* are in the Indiana State Library and have John Kimberlin's signature in pencil on them.

By 1815 Lexington had its first hotel, and the Indiana Manufacturing Company was formed. This was actually the territory's second bank. It was short lived because of unscrupulous loan practices.[11] As the first half of the new decade passed, Lexington boasted a general store, a blacksmith, a tailor, a coach house, and a house painter.[12] The house painter is particularly significant because his presence documents that clapboard homes were starting to appear in the area. The era of the log cabin was not gone, but wealthier residents were beginning to move to multiroom frame homes. Within two years, Lexington had its first school.

Other than gristmills, the primary manufacturing in the Lexington area was a salt spring on the New London road one mile east of town. Briney water was boiled to extract the salt which was sold for $2 per bushel for preserving food.[13]

With statehood in 1816 came a state capital in Corydon, only fifty-five miles away, and a settlement boom across the new state. The land office at Vincennes was briefly the busiest in the nation, selling 286,000 acres in 1817, and Indiana's birth rate was among the highest in the world.[14]

Despite the population growth and the sprouting of commercial establishments near the Kimberlin homestead, the local economy lagged far behind that of its more prosperous neighbors to the south in New Albany and to the east in Madison. The *Western Eagle* ceased publication in January 1816, with a melancholy note from its editor that read, "partly for want of support, but mostly owing to the negligence of those in arrears, I am compelled to discontinue the *Western Eagle*."[15] A new newspaper, the *Cornucopia of the West*, began publication in Lexington in June 1816; it lasted eight weeks. From then to the early 1850s, Lexington and Scott County had no local newspaper to document the area's economy, politics, or social life. The Kimberlins and their neighbors continued to depend on nearby Madison for most of their news and much of their trade.

New County, New Promise

Scott County was established by the Indiana General Assembly on February 1, 1820.[16] The previous decade had seen the population of Indiana grow from 24,000 inhabitants to 147,000.[17] Census takers counted 2,335 people in Scott County, including 1,250 free white males, 1,062 free white females, six freed "colored" people, and eleven foreigners.[18] The small foreign-born population showed the relative isolation of Scott County compared to its neighbors along the Ohio River. The majority of Scott County residents were of southern origin. Their intermarriage (Daniel Kimberlin's marriage to Ursula Brinton was the first recorded marriage in what would become Scott County) strengthened those ties and acted to maintain a purity of southern bloodlines that had a lasting impact.

The economy of Scott County in 1820 was overwhelmingly agricultural. The census recorded only "heads of households" and all data

related to these mostly white males. Of this category, 444 men were
engaged in agriculture, eighteen in commerce, and sixty-two worked in
manufacturing.[19] Scott County's manufacturing base consisted of a couple
of mills that were "in good order, demand and sales dull."[20] In one mill,
two men and "one boy or girl" earned a total of $200 in wages in the previ-
ous year.[21] A "crockery establishment new and in good condition, demand
considerable, and sales rapid," employed one man at $40 per year, and a
larger meal and flour mill employed twenty-three men, two boys, and two
girls for a total of $2,073 wages the previous year.[22] We do not know if

MICHAEL B. MURPHY

Abraham Kimberlin

either of the mills belonged to the
Kimberlins, but we do know that
Abraham and Daniel Kimberlin,
the eldest sons of John, operated
a mill together on a branch of
Kimberlin Creek near what is now
known as Beswick Chapel Cemetery, on land owned by Abraham.

Together, the brothers supported twenty-five people on their
homesteads, including four slaves.
According to the 1820 census,
Abraham owned one male slave
fourteen to twenty-six years of
age, and a female slave no older
than forty-five. Daniel owned one
male and one female, each under
fourteen years old. The Kimberlin

slaves, if reported accurately, represent two-thirds of the slaves accounted
for in Scott County in the 1820 census. This is peculiar because, while the
Kimberlins were certainly the earliest established family in the area, there
is no evidence that they were the wealthiest. We do not know the eventual
fate of the Kimberlin slaves. They do not appear in the 1830 census, and
there is no other written documentation in family letters. However, in the
1850 census, the first to name individuals, a James W. Collins is listed as
a resident of Abraham's household. Kimberlin family legend holds that
this man is one and the same as "Collins," a slave owned by Abraham in
the 1830s.

Public policy initiatives by the Indiana legislature in Corydon had a direct and immediate impact on the Scott County economy almost from its beginning. The state declared the Brushy Fork of the Muscatatuck River and the lower reaches of Stucker Creek to be public highways. This meant that public money could be spent to maintain them as navigable streams, and that the Kimberlins and their neighbors would have more reliable routes for transporting their milled goods to markets along the Ohio River when the water was up.

At some point in the 1820s, Abraham established a tannery on property he owned on the northern edge of the bog owned by his father. The bog was roughly a half mile northwest of the modern village of Nabb, originally named Griswold. It produced enough spring flow to satisfy the water-intensive needs of a tannery (and still provides the household water supply for a family descended from the Kimberlins).

By this time, Abraham was in his forties and supported eleven people in his household, including eight children under the age of twenty. The small business provided income for his family, as well as a gathering spot for local farmers to exchange news of the day. But maybe most important, Abraham, like other pioneer merchants, was one of what historian James H. Madison calls the "essential middlemen, performing a variety of services necessary to move Indiana [and Scott County] beyond self-sufficient agriculture."[23]

The Kimberlin Ledger

The Kimberlin merchant operation was not limited to a tannery. On the same site, Abraham also operated an alehouse and a general store. A man visiting the site south of Lexington could buy everything from bacon to nails to medicine. Credit was given and accounts held open because customers often paid on a seasonal basis with the produce of their own hard work.

Abraham was a detailed but sporadic record keeper who wrote his transactions in a leather-bound ledger to which this writer is grateful to have access. Not all of his records survive, but the family has preserved business records covering a four-year span from 1837 to 1841. There are inexplicable gaps in the records that would not be acceptable by today's business standards, and there is no written justification for why Abraham noted the transactions that he did. Nevertheless, the ledger provides a fascinating window into the commercial life and the daily needs of Scott County residents during that period.

Reading the original strokes of his pen, fueled by the gooseberry ink that was produced nearby, one can visualize the flow of customers and the contents of the shelves as he wrote: "Feburary 16, 1837- Joseph Cole, 75 cents for 2 ½ bushels of corn at 30 cents/bushel,"[24] and on April 12, 1839: "Hyatt one pack of sweet potato seed 37 cents." The Kimberlin ledger documents dates, names, the nature of the transaction, prices for products, debts paid, and sometimes a promise of work to be done. One page, for example, contains the following entries (typed verbatim, including gaps, misspellings, and abbreviations):

> May Washington Daily one pair of half soles for shoes 12 ½ cents
>
> 19th Jacob Jackson for carding 13 ½ pds of wool $1.12
>
> 23rd John Daly 13 ½ pds bacon at 8 ⅓ cents a pd $1.12
>
> 23rd John Daly wheel wright? 12 ½ cents Dr. A. Ollers one vial of .....12 ½ cents Dr. Hyatt 12 ½ cents worth of laudum Sept 14th Dr. Hyatt bushel of appels
>
> 25th John Bower ....32 cents
>
> 26th Elizabeth Camper......
>
> 26th Dr. Hyatt extracting a tooth 25 cents
>
> 27th Dr. Hyatt 12 ½ cents for calomel
>
> 27th William Harmon 13 ¾ pds of bacon at 8 ⅓ cent per pound $1.14
>
> Oct 3rd Abraham Kimberlin 12 ½ cents
>
> 14th Elizabeth Camper for weaving 12 ¾ yds of blanketing at 16+cents per yard 1 12.5 cents
>
> 13th John Daly 7 ¼ pds of bacon at 8 ⅓ cents a pd $1.06

The entries in Abraham's ledger provide some of the earliest known documentation of commercial life in Scott County. For example, Abraham's children provided some of the labor for his business. In a May 1838 ledger entry, Abraham noted: "Washington Daly for a pair of half soles for shoes by the hand of Washington Kimberlin 12 ½ cents." On September 11, 1840, Abraham jotted: "Jacob Kimberlin one days hauling . . . Jacob Kimberlin 50 cents." We also know that neighbors were allowed to

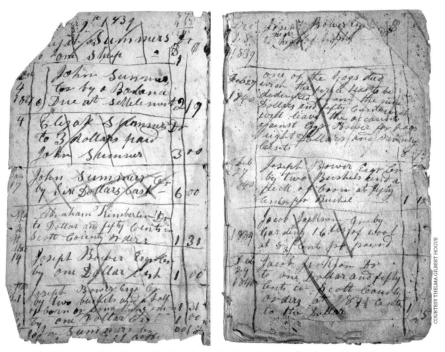

A set of pages from the original leather-bound ledger kept by Abraham Kimberlin for his businesses.

work off debts in his store. In July 1839 Abraham wrote: "John Summers three days work $1.50. . . . John Summers right to a part of the money 31 cents." The Kimberlin tannery and general store also acted as a "job shop" for nearby residents who had services to sell to their neighbors. On June 10, 1839, Abraham paid Joseph Fisher "37 cents for making a plow beam," and paid Mrs. John Daly in November, 1837 for "mending a pair of pants."

Abraham's ledger also shows that he acted as a middleman for collecting and paying out government notes. On April 25, 1839, Abraham noted: "Abraham Kimberlin $4 paid to . . . I.N. White agent of the surplus revenues." In June 1841 Abraham accepted $1.50 from Jacob Jackson for "Scott Co. orders," and seems to have given Joseph Bower $1 cash for Scott County orders valued at $1.31. On December 14, 1840, Abraham apparently discounted Scott County orders to John Summers, noting: "John Summers $1.80 in Scott Co. orders 75 cents to one dollar." Abraham kept track of his own personal transactions as well. On October 10, 1840, he paid "64 cents for one pair of shoe welts" and later paid himself fifty

cents "for one days work at framing a tan vat." On February 16, 1837, he
simply noted: "personal transaction $5.61."

Thanks to Abraham's ledger, and his descendants' efforts to preserve
it, we can appreciate the value Scott County residents of the 1830s and
1840s must have put on material items. The going rate for common labor
reasonably seems to have been fifty cents per day, based on Abraham's
entries for a variety of work performed. Considering that a pulled tooth
cost half a day's labor, and three pounds of coffee cost a full day's labor,
one can see how health care and coffee were considered luxuries.

In a larger sense, Abraham's ledger confirms that as late as 1841, the
Scott County economy was, for the most part, an economy based on local-
ly produced goods and services. The transition from subsistence economy
to an agricultural/commercial economy had clearly been made, but Scott
County was not yet participating in the regional or national economy like
its neighbors along the Ohio River. Scott County's economic profile more
closely resembled those counties in the state's more isolated interior.
Still, significant progress toward what historian James H. Madison calls
"the single most important public goal" of the antebellum era had been
achieved—that is breaking down isolation among Hoosiers.[25]

Kimberlins Have Company

As Hoosier pioneers began to trade with people beyond their immediate horizons, the number of trading centers also multiplied. These
represented the first commercial centers that required investment and
rudimentary marketing. The Kimberlin tannery/alehouse/general store
northwest of Nabb would have operated much like the other six dry goods
stores in Scott County in 1840.[26] Combined, they represented nearly
$5,000 in capital investment.[27] Joining the general stores were twelve
mills and three furniture makers. The agricultural economy was still based
on corn (52,000 bushels), wheat (15,000 bushels), and pork (4,600 swine
compared to 3,600 sheep and 2,600 cattle).[28] Most of the corn not used
for family needs was used for animal feed.

The three sons of the Kimberlin patriarch, John, were still the primary support for the entire Kimberlin clan in 1840. In addition to Abraham,
Daniel was co-owner of a small mill, while Isaac was a farmer. In all, they
provided for thirty-nine Kimberlins in three homesteads, all within a one-

mile triangle.[29] By today's markers, Isaac farmed the original homestead on both sides of Westport Road; Abraham lived just north of the bog that still exists; and Daniel farmed property just west of current State Road 3.

By the early 1840s, farming for the Kimberlins and their neighbors became more productive as wood plows began to give way to steel plows. Steel could be sharpened, and thus cut through the silt loam of Scott County more efficiently. Cattle were not the fattened bovines of today's farms. The Scott County cattle were long-legged, long-haired, and long-horned livestock. Similarly, the Scott County swine were ridge-rooters who foraged on the open range. These original razorbacks were not improved upon until breeding became popular after 1850, when transportation of livestock became more practicable.

Transportation from Trails to Railroads

When the Kimberlins made their trek from the landing on the Ohio River at what would become Madison in 1805, they followed a Shawnee Indian trail that reached west across broad meadows and small creeks and eventually connected with the north-south Three Notch Trail that stretched from the Falls of the Ohio to Fall Creek at present-day Indianapolis. The trail was nothing more than a footpath, not fit for wheeled vehicles, and certainly not capable of serving as a conduit for driving animals. The Cincinnati Trace, begun in 1799, was farther to the north and served primarily as a supply route between the two largest towns in the area, Cincinnati and Vincennes.

Rivers and creeks, particularly the Muscatatuck River in what would be northern Scott County, and Stucker and Kimberlin Creeks were the primary means for moving bulk items until 1821, when the Indiana legislature passed its first highway act.[30] The legislature envisioned a system of roads that would facilitate the movement of people, livestock, and freight north from the Ohio River to Lake Michigan, and west from Cincinnati to Lafayette, Vincennes, and Fort Wayne.

Indian trails were soon being improved to serve as legitimate roads, and Scott County benefited. The Charlestown road, following a Shawnee trail from Vallonia to Springville on the Ohio River opened a north-south route, while the Vienna road, heading west from Lexington to Vienna and Salem, and east to Madison, created a substantial east-west route. In the

Isaac Kimberlin

MADISON AND INDIANAPOLIS

RAIL ROAD.

The Madison and Indianapolis Rail Road Company, having this day taken possession of the Rail Road under the authority of a late Act of the General Assembly, now respectfully announce to the public, and especially travellers and business men, that the Line will be kept in operation, for the conveyance of travellers and freight, every day in the week, except Sundays, and under the personal care of experienced and attentive men. It will be the ambition of the Company that the high reputation of the Rail Road, from no accident having ever occurred on it, shall be maintained. Strict attention will be given to the comfort of travellers, and the careful and prompt delivery of freight.

The Directors have established a tariff of tolls for all the leading points from Madison to Columbus, upon a scale as low, it is believed, as any road in the West; and which is so arranged as to encourage and facilitate the trade and exportation of the surplus of the country. The board hope to have the road extended to Columbus, so as to convey passengers and freight to and from that point by the month of June next.

Until the road shall be completed to Scipio, the rate of tolls on *freight*, from the depot, (at Griffith's) will be the same as heretofore charged by the State, except that instead of taking State Scrip, as heretofore, all payments will be required in par funds, subject, however, to a deduction of twenty-five per cent. from the nominal charges.

The Board of Directors having, in their efforts to extend the road, contracted large debts in the purchase of Iron, are compelled, from necessity, to require the tolls to be paid in par funds, which only will discharge such indebtedness.

The Directors and Stockholders having embarked, with much present sacrifice and hazard, in the effort to extend this great work, so indispensable to the interests of the country, appeal with confidence to their fellow citizens for patronage and acquiescence in the policy adopted by the Board in the administration of the operations of the road.

The Board feel assured, that a community so deeply interested in the extension of the road, will readily perceive that whatever prospers the Company, will hasten the extension and final completion of the whole Line, as to this object the arrangements and energies of the Company are and will be earnestly directed, as fast, as by the expected aid of their fellow citizens, and the income of the road, they shall be enabled.

N. B. PALMER, Pres't.

MADISON, Feb. 18, 1843.

Madison and Indianapolis Rail Road Co.

PRINTED AT THE OFFI

INDIANA STATE

Broadside announcing the opening of business for the Madison and Indianapolis Railroad, the first of its kind in the state. The broadside promises: "Strict attention will be given to the comfort of travelers, and the careful and prompt delivery of freight."

next decade, the Michigan Road, stretching from Madison to Michigan City, was finished in 1836.

The roads were paid for and maintained by a mixture of state and local road taxes. Residents could satisfy their local tax obligation by volunteering three days of work each year for local road maintenance. Counties were divided into road maintenance districts, and the supervisor of each district stood for election. The Kimberlins, and their cousins the Whitlachs (The name is frequently spelled Whitlatch in family letters and government archival material. The author has chosen to use Whitlach for consistency.) served as both road district supervisors and as named members of maintenance crews. Scott County had as many as eleven road districts at any one time, and given the critical nature of well-maintained roads, the position of road supervisor was significant within the community.

The Indiana legislature broadened its commitment to transportation in 1836, when it passed an internal improvement bill that mirrored contemporary efforts by Whig politicians at the federal level. The Indiana bill authorized spending $10 million for macadamized roads, three canals, river navigational improvements, and the chartering of railroads that were conspicuously absent from the state.

The canal craze bypassed Scott County; the nearest canal was the Whitewater, to the north and east. Railroad companies, however, were sprouting almost as fast as investors could be found. The first major railroad near Scott County was the Madison to Indianapolis route that reached Indianapolis in 1847. This route was particularly significant because it connected two of Indiana's three largest cities (New Albany being the third).[31] Farmers and small manufacturers now had access to both the Ohio River and ports beyond and to the deep interior of a state that was filling in quickly with people. By 1850 Indiana had eight cities with populations of more than 2,500 inhabitants, and the Kimberlins and other Scott County traders and farmers were beneficiaries. Another railroad, the Ohio and Indianapolis, chartered by the general assembly in February 1846,[32] sliced through Scott County by way of Lexington, making the county seat a transportation hub for the new era. This railroad was known as the "Calico Road" because workers were paid in dry goods.

Technology Comes to Commerce

By 1850 southern Indiana had lost its dominance over the state to central and northern Indiana. Immigration to the Ohio River counties slowed while population exploded in South Bend, Fort Wayne, Richmond, Lafayette, and Indianapolis. With the population boom came people with inventive minds and entrepreneurial spirits. The Oliver family, for example, settled in South Bend and invented the chilled plow, which became one of the most significant agricultural technology advancements of the mid-nineteenth century. The advantage of the chilled plow over plain steel or wooden plows was that dirt was less likely to clump on the plow, which made plowing faster and more efficient. It also did not break when it struck rocks.

Also in the early part of the decade, reapers reached Scott County. These were two-man operations that allowed mechanized harvesting for the first time. Concurrent with the arrival of reapers was the two-horse grain drill, which, for those who could afford it, eliminated the primitive and labor-intensive practice of broadcasting seed by hand. The grain drill, followed within a few years by the two-row grain drill, also saved farmers valuable seed by ensuring the best possible start for each individual seed.[33]

These advancements in agriculture technology, and the popularization of selective breeding of pigs and cattle, may have been enough for Abraham to leave the tannery business and return exclusively to farming. The 1850 census lists Abraham, now sixty-eight years old, working as a full-time farmer for the first time since the 1820 census.[34] The 1850 census is particularly helpful in tracking both Kimberlin and Scott County progress because it is the first census to enumerate all individuals by name and to list the occupations of all males over the age of fifteen.

While we do not know exactly why Abraham abandoned commerce, we do know that all Kimberlin households except John B., a cooper, in the county were engaged exclusively in farming. We also know that Abraham had taken in his widowed daughter, Nancy Williams, and that she and her forty-two-year old son, Absolum, were classified as "insane," two of only three "insane" citizens of Lexington Township. The value of Abraham's land is not listed.

The wealthiest Kimberlin in 1850 seems to have been Isaac, who owned land valued at $1,500, according to the census. For some reason, the Kimberlin clan did not keep pace economically with the significant growth in assets that many other Scott County residents realized. Isaac's holdings, for example, represented only 0.6 of 1 percent of the total reported land value of $241,600 for the township.[35] While the Kimberlins were returning to agriculture, their neighbors, particularly in Lexington, were turning more and more to commerce. The decision by the Kimberlin "heads of household" to stay on their farms may have been as varied as their individual personalities, but one can conclude that their farm income was sufficient to support a sizable brood. The long-term economic implications for the family were that their relative wealth could only grow or shrink with the agricultural economy.

The Kimberlins' failure to multiply their assets during the decade of the 1840s reflects a concentration of commercial power in new urban centers, where customers gathered and a critical mass of retail products and services could be accessed in one location. The town of Lexington boasted a variety of ongoing business concerns in 1850. A visitor could avail himself of the services of seven merchants, four physicians, twelve lawyers, four carpenters, three tanners (a former Kimberlin trade), three chair makers, and lesser numbers of virtually every trade an antebellum Hoosier could need.

The apparent static nature of the Kimberlins' fortunes may have had more to do with a lifestyle choice than anything else. Most of the Kimberlin men were educated for their time. Extant letters display a mastery of grammar and sentence structure, forgiving the occasional local colloquialism. Certainly, they were better prepared to face the future than a majority of their neighbors. Only 25 percent of Scott County residents were reported to have a record of attending school in 1850, and 15 percent were reported as illiterate.[36]

The English Influence

While the Kimberlins were holding their own, the English family of Lexington was becoming a dominant force in Scott County's economy. The father/son combination of E. G. and William English held real estate valued at $15,000 in 1850, by far the wealthiest land interest in the county. The English family was a relative latecomer to what would become Scott County, if measured on the Kimberlin timeline. Like many Hoosiers, the English family migration pattern came from the East (Delaware) through Virginia, then through Kentucky in the late 1790s. The English family members were in the line of the Eustises, who were intermarried with the Faquhars and Lees. Elisha English's maternal grandfather was a member of the Fourth Virginia Regiment in the American Revolution.[37] Elisha married Mahala Eastin, descendant of Jost Hite, one of the earliest settlers of the Shenandoah Valley in Virginia, in Lexington, Indiana, in 1819. Elisha held a variety of political posts early in his career. He was constable for Lexington Township,[38] a two-term sheriff of Scott County, and served for twenty years, off and on, in the Indiana General Assembly. An active Democrat, English also served as vice president of the Democratic National Convention in 1848 and as the U.S. Marshal for Indiana during President James Buchanan's administration.[39]

English's notoriety, however, came from his real estate deals in Scott County. While he started well behind early pioneers such as the Kimberlins in the amount of land he owned, English had a knack for real estate that eventually allowed him to become one of the chief farmland and livestock financiers in the county. When farmers could not make payments on debt owed to English, he took over title to the land or livestock, building his wealth on the backs of his neighbors.

English's aggregation of land and money served as a fortuitous set up for his even more ambitious son, William H., born in Lexington on August 27, 1822. Like most of the Kimberlins, English was educated at local Lexington schools. Unlike most of his neighbors, however, English went on to study at Hanover College in Madison for three years. The Hanover experience allowed him to pass the bar in 1840 at the age of eighteen and to begin practicing law in Lexington, the county seat.

Portrait of Indiana congressman William H. English from the Thirty-fifth Congress, which met from March 4, 1857, to March 4, 1859, the first two years of James Buchanan's presidency.

William also quickly began to move up the ladder in Democratic politics. He served as a delegate to the Democrat State Convention in 1840 and was appointed postmaster of Lexington in 1842 by President John Tyler. English was appointed Clerk of the Indiana House of Representatives in 1843, and, for helping Jesse Bright attain one of Indiana's U.S. Senate seats, was appointed a clerk in the second auditor's office of the U.S. Treasury Department by President James K. Polk in 1847.[40]

English invested much of his $1,400 annual auditor's salary in the public debt of Texas. He sold futures to his fellow clerks, and when they could not meet payments, he took title to the futures and kept their money.[41] English's shrewdness helped him build assets until the election of Whig Zachary Taylor as president in 1848 sent him back to Scott County without a job.

English was not idle long. Almost immediately upon his return to Lexington, he began renewing his political connections and planning his eventual rise in the Indiana Democratic Party. In 1850 English served as secretary to the Indiana Constitutional Convention. In 1851–52, he served one term in the Indiana House of Representatives and was elected speaker for that term. In 1853 English replaced Cyrus Dunham as the congressman from Indiana's Second District, which included Clark, Jefferson, Floyd, and Scott Counties. English's victory was only the second time since 1843 that Scott County had voted for a Democrat for Congress, breaking forever the Whigs' successful run in the county.

The Kimberlins' Fortunes Slip

The English business machine was running full throttle during the 1850s, increasing the combined wealth of the English family in Scott County from $15,000 (including real estate) to $103,000 (including real estate). Personal property (listed for the first time in the 1860 census) for the father-son team added another $36,000 in asset value. Mortgage lending and their neighbors' inability to keep up with payments clearly had been financially lucrative for the Englishes.[42]

Meanwhile, the Kimberlins regressed in the 1850s. Farming continued to be almost their exclusive occupation. Milton Kimberlin, a forty-one-year-old farmer with a wife and eight children, appears to have been the wealthiest Kimberlin at the end of the decade, with combined assets valued at $2,800. This was nearly a doubling of Milton's wealth since 1850. Other Kimberlins, for example, Isaac, saw the value of their assets dip slightly in the 1850s.[43]

Abraham, the Kimberlin pioneer in commerce, was crippled in a violent attack in 1858, allegedly at the hands of his own daughter, Manerva Jane. The *Lexington Clipper* reported in its September 23, 1858, edition under the headline "HORRIBLE," that someone "struck the old gentleman while in bed, a severe blow with an axe, on the head, penetrating the brain . . . the axe was found next morning in the yard covered with blood . . . his own daughter has been arrested and tried before Squire Campbell and for want of bail was lodged in our jail to await her trial at the next term of the Circuit Court."[44] Court records for that term, held in February 1859, have disappeared from the Scott County Courthouse and are not available for review. Abraham actually survived the brain injury and moved in with his daughter, Sarah, and her husband, James Reed, in Wood Township, Clark County, Indiana.[45] Abraham died in 1860 at the home of another daughter, Lucinda, who was married to Silas Allhands.

The divergence between the Kimberlin and English fortunes may ultimately have been caused by the English family's ability to adapt better to changing social conditions. As the nascent commercial centers formed in Scott County in the 1840s, they reinforced natural human desire to congregate and socialize. The combination of available products and services with a social population with disposable income was a death blow to the trading-post tradition that had survived in Scott County since its inception. The only commercial enterprises that survived in rural areas generally were mills and other businesses tied directly to raw agricultural products or a source of power, such as a stream.

In addition to the commercial center and county seat of Lexington, the towns of Austin, Vienna, and Scottsburg were beginning to grow. The establishment of Scottsburg along the north-south Louisville to Indianapolis railroad created a rivalry between this railroad town and the more established Lexington for economic primacy. The citizens of Scottsburg tried several times to shift the county seat away from Lexington, but as the 1860s dawned Lexington maintained its role as government and economic hub of the county.

About this time, farmers discovered that the soil of Scott County was nearly perfect for growing tomatoes—a crop that helped diversify the

LIBRARY OF CONGRESS

Campaign flyer for the successful 1860 Republican Party ticket of Abraham Lincoln of Illinois for president and Hannibal Hamlin of Maine for vice president.

county's farm economy and offered a new harvest season that was not aligned with traditional cash crops such as corn, hay, and oats.

Railroads had brought greater ease of freight shipment deeper into the county. Macadamized roads provided almost weather-proof access to railroad terminals. Livestock and grain could be sent to market fresher.Railroads were a mixed bag for the farmers of Scott County. With the ease of transportation came a new class of businessman, and a new dynamic that gained in economic influence over the next forty years. Railroad companies faced little competition for access to distant markets such as Chicago and the northeast. Rail-roads could name their price, and the only alternative for bulk goods was the seventeen-mile overland route to the Ohio River and a slow flatboat ride downriver. Livestock could still be driven to Cincinnati, or to a ferry at Louisville.

As economic tension between Lexington and Scottsburg festered, national political and economic issues threatened to upset what seemed like a bright future for Scott County. The presidential election of 1860 saw Indiana and its thirteen electoral votes go for Abraham Lincoln. The Republican candidate had a plurality in Scott County, but the county cast more total votes for Lincoln's opponents (660 for Lincoln, 447 for Ste-phen Douglas, 262 for John Breckinridge, and 52 for John Bell).[46] Scott County voters had stayed with their familial roots, but more importantly sent a signal that in the growing debate over secession, their sentiments looked to the South as well.

As tension between North and South erupted into open warfare in 1861, traffic downriver came to a standstill. Prices for agricultural goods dropped, and the entire Ohio valley slid into an economic depression.[47] In

Louisville, the hub of this regional economy, the population dropped by 10,000, and sixty-eight of seventy jobbing houses (equivalent of today's distribution warehouse) closed during 1861–62. Ninety-five of 112 banks in Illinois closed in 1861 alone.[48] Indiana banks were devastated by the war because they had invested heavily in Southern state bonds. Those bonds were now worthless.[49] While prices at market were depressed, the cost of transporting midwestern grain rose. Railroads, controlled by New England business interests, nearly tripled their rates for moving products to markets in the East.[50] Southern Indiana merchants and farmers "complained bitterly against the obstruction of their river outlets, and defiantly engaged in contraband trade with the South."[51] They established an "elaborate system" of off-loading cargo in Madison, then transferring it by skiff to Smithland, Kentucky, then to the Louisville and Nashville Railroad, and on to Memphis.[52]

The economic depression caused frustration and resentment among southern Indiana merchants that was directed toward the northeast. Newspapers such as the *New Albany Weekly Ledger* wrote blazing editorials, blaming currency depreciation and business stagnation on "fanatical, abolitionized, canting, hypocritical New England states."[53] Even the Republican *Indianapolis Journal* editorialized that concessions should be made to the South in order to keep the Ohio valley unified.[54] The town of Loogootee in Martin County was described by one businessman as a deserted village. "Everything in Southern Indiana is prostrated," he said.[55]

Politicians played on the natural fears of their constituents and the economic pain caused by the blockade by giving incendiary speeches for personal gain. Of course, this was no surprise. Scott County's position as part of a Northern state, but populated largely by immigrants from and descendants of the Virginia/Kentucky tradition, put its citizens squarely on the fault line of the growing national fissure. The county's politicians had had one foot on each side of the divide since the days of Andrew Jackson.

3

Scott County Political Traditions

Kimberlin family members were firsthand witnesses to, and occasional participants in, the electoral process in the new state of Indiana. Kimberlins who met the legal requirements of being a free white male, at least twenty-one years old, a citizen, and a resident of the state at least one year were, like nearly all of their neighbors, of the Jeffersonian Republican tradition.[1] Most Hoosiers prior to 1820 brought this philosophy of agrarian independence with them from the valleys of Virginia, through the Cumberland Gap into Kentucky, and eventually across the Ohio River to the land opened up to settlement after the Treaty of Grouseland in 1805.[2]

The first election in Indiana was held August 5, 1816. Official returns have not been found, leaving historians to rely primarily upon contemporary newspaper accounts. In the race for governor, Jonathan Jennings is generally credited with garnering 5,211 votes to Thomas Posey's 3,934 votes from the estimated 12,112 eligible voters.[3] Christopher Harrison was elected lieutenant governor, and Waller Taylor and James Noble were elected by the legislature as the state's first U.S. Senators. Indiana was initially granted one representative by Congress and William Hendricks was chosen after a five-week campaign.

It is difficult to imagine with a twenty-first-century mind the limited nature of electioneering at the dawn of Indiana. Candidates campaigned by allowing someone to report in a local newspaper that they might be drafted to run. In turn, it was routine for the candidate to deny his availability until he could resist no longer. Electioneering was frowned upon so handbills served as the only outlet for a candidate's views. The Kimberlin hometown of Lexington played an influential role in early state politics because it was also home to one of only four printing presses in the entire state. Therefore, all ambitious politicians had to do business in Lexington.

The election of Jennings, Noble, and Hendricks established a powerful triumvirate that dominated Indiana politics until the early 1830s. Jennings and Hendricks played political musical chairs, prompting complaints of an "elected aristocracy," but throughout those early years three issues seemed to be a constant: internal improvements, a reduction in the price of public land, and banking policy.

The first indication historians have of southern Indiana electoral sentiment is the returns for the lone congressional seat in 1817. Hendricks defeated Posey in Clark County, which then encompassed the Kimberlin homesteads, and also in Jefferson County, consistent with the statewide result.[4] Clark and Jefferson Counties again followed statewide sentiment in the first contested gubernatorial election in 1819. Jennings defeated his lieutenant governor, Harrison, in both counties and across Indiana.[5] The Kimberlins' record of public service first surfaces in 1820, the year Scott County was created as an offshoot of Clark County. Daniel and Isaac Kimberlin were sworn in as grand jurors, both being described as "good and lawful men."[6] Both men were farmers near Lexington.

The first real political contest in Indiana was the 1824 presidential canvass. In just eight years politics had gained a measure of sophistication in the state. Stump speaking became a popular venue for communicating with voters, and political parties began to take shape. In that era, the state election was held in August, and federal officeholders were elected in November. In Indiana Henry Clay backers were mostly businessmen and well-to-do farmers, while lawyers and professional men supported John Quincy Adams. Poor farmers and young men tended to ally with Andrew Jackson, and William Crawford had virtually no support. Jackson's margins over his rivals in Indiana—2,123 more votes than Clay and 4,351 more than Adams—proved to be similar to the rest of the country.[7] When the presidential election was thrown into the House of Representatives, Indiana's vote went to Jackson.

Scott County's first opportunity to participate in a presidential election, and its first step toward establishing a political tradition of its own, occurred in 1824. The county went for Jackson (123 votes to 84 for Clay and 26 for Adams), although Scott County did not send any delegates to a state Jackson convention at Salem, Indiana.[8] The big issue that year

LIBRARY OF CONGRESS

Cartoon titled "A Foot Race" spoofs the 1824 presidential election. A crowd of cheering citizens watch as candidates (left to right) John Quincy Adams, William Crawford, and Andrew Jackson stride toward the finish.

was whether elected representatives should consider themselves to be "instructed," that is direct representatives of the people, or whether they were "delegated representatives," with the discretion to use their judgment. Generally speaking, the Whigs believed in delegation, while the Democrats supported "right of instruction."

The political dynamics of the area that made up the new second congressional district (Indiana gained two more congressional seats as a result of the 1820 census) also first became evident that year. Scott and Clark Counties emerged as consistently Democratic. Their dominant neighbor Jefferson County, with its county seat, Madison, the largest city in Indiana, began to lay its claim as a Whig county, going for Clay.[9]

Scott County voters also began to show a tendency toward fickleness. Former governor and then current congressman Jennings was popular in Scott County from 1816, when he became the first governor, through his election as the first second district congressman in 1822. Scott County voters flipped on Jennings in 1824, however, favoring Jeremiah Sullivan of nearby Madison by a margin of more than 200 votes. Jennings prevailed, however, carrying enough votes district-wide to defeat Sullivan. Eighteen twenty-four was a watershed year in Indiana and Scott County because it marked the evolution from Jeffersonian to Jacksonian philosophies. The Jeffersonian ideals promoted democracy only to a point. The masses should vote, but public office should be reserved for the educated class. Jacksonian ideals suggested that democracy meant the masses were equally capable of serving in office.[10]

Following the 1824 presidential race, Jackson forces in Indiana turned to local organizing and began to dominate races for county and township offices. In pre-Civil War Indiana, the office of supervisor of roads was one of the most important local positions because good roads were critical to a farmer's ability to get his crops to market, and to conduct virtually all commerce. Supervisors were required to list the names of their "crew members." The names usually included a healthy dose of family members and the jobs became the first real form of what we know today as political patronage in Indiana.

The Kimberlins and their cousins, the Whitlachs, frequently served as supervisors of roads in Lexington Township, Scott County. Original election poll books and tally sheets for Lexington Township document the names of extended Kimberlin family members voting, holding elective office, and serving as precinct judges and inspectors from 1826 to 1867.[11] Voting prior to 1826 took place at the county courthouse or the home of a prominent citizen rather than at precinct polling stations. Ironically, one of the primary reasons voting locations were dispersed was to diffuse the drinking and fighting that was notorious at county polling locations. The *Corydon Gazette* editorialized on August 8, 1822, after a particularly rowdy election day, that the legislature should ban drinking on Election Day and move voting to the townships.

The period between the presidential elections of 1824 and 1828 also served as the transition between candidacies of nonaligned politicians, and politicians who were the creation of political parties. James Brown Ray was the last governor chosen without the support of a party when he defeated Isaac Newton Blackford in 1825. Scott County went for Ray by a margin of just twenty votes.[12] Ray was also the first gubernatorial candidate to publicly announce his candidacy in person rather than allowing third parties to draft him.[13]

By 1828 the Jackson and Adams forces were gelling into true party organizations, though without broadly accepted given names. Adams backers were generally assumed to belong to the Administration Party. Ray was able one last time to hold off these nascent parties, defeating the Jackson man, Israel Canby, by 2,880 votes, and the Adams man, Harbin

Moore, by 4,233 votes.[14] Scott County, in a rare tandem with Jefferson County, backed Ray, while Clark County went heavily for Canby.

The Jeffersonian Republican tradition completed its evolution into the Jacksonian Democratic tradition in the 1828 presidential election. Indiana went once again for Jackson, and so did Scott and Clark Counties. Jefferson County gave Adams the advantage by a mere twenty votes out of more than 1,300 cast. Jefferson County continued to overshadow Scott County in the pure number of votes cast, however, 1,336 to 430.[15]

In 1831 Indiana's congressional elections were shifted to odd years. At the same time, the 1830 census results caused Indiana's congressional delegation to more than double, to seven seats. Interest in serving in Congress spiked in the second district, and six men submitted their names for election. John Carr, a former sheriff of Clark County, won easily with Scott and Clark Counties going with the winner and Jefferson County going nearly two to one for William W. Wick.[16]

Although official party labels for candidates were still three years away, Noah Noble led the Whig Party to victory in that year's gubernatorial election. For the first time, none of the three primary counties in the second congressional district picked the winner. Scott and Clark Counties, true to their habit, went for James Read, the Jacksonian Democrat, while Jefferson County backed Milton Stapp, known as an independent.[17]

The 1830s in Indiana, much like the 1850s, was a decade of shifting political tides and loyalties. As political parties took formal shape in Indiana, Scott County voters began to move away from their rock-ribbed Jacksonian principles to a new form of pragmatism that was also symptomatic of a developing divide among people who had voted in lockstep for nearly twenty years. These first rumblings of a dissonance in the country grew into open struggle during the next thirty years as the issues that led to the Civil War caused splits among established parties and the formation of new parties.

The first election in Indiana in which candidates ran under the banner of a true political party was the 1832 presidential election. Jackson, the standard-bearer of the new Democratic Party formed the year before, took Indiana by significant margins, with Scott and Clark Counties backing Jackson two to one over Clay, the candidate of the National Republicans (not to be confused with the modern Republican Party, formed twenty years later). The Anti-Mason Party, led in Indiana by Jennings's brother-in-law, David Mitchell of Corydon, nominated William Wirt, but he received only twenty-seven votes spread among six counties. Wirt did not receive any votes in Scott County.[18]

The driving issue in southern Indiana that year was the establishment of state bank charters. Jackson had revoked the charter of the Second Bank of the United States, which had branches in Louisville and Cincinnati. Businessmen in southern Indiana were looking for access to capital and to convenient banking relationships. Scott County voters chose to replace their state representative, John Harrod, with Elisha English that year, but because party labels were not yet in use for legislative races, it is impossible to tell if the banking issue was a direct cause of the switch. There was no newspaper in Scott County at that time, and the *Madison Courier* did not report on the legislative races. The first congressional election held with party-labeled candidates occurred in 1833. Scott County had been redistricted into the new third district, but the result was the same. The incumbent, Carr, running under the Democratic banner was one of six Democrats to win that

A campaign portrait of General Andrew Jackson issued during the presidential election of 1828. An oval bust portrait of Jackson is surrounded by the words "Protector & Defender of Beauty & Booty." Orleans at the bottom refers to Jackson's spectacular War of 1812 victory at New Orleans.

year. National Republicans won only one seat (second district), and that was by two votes.[19]

By 1834 a two-party system was fully formed in Indiana. The Whigs in Indiana were a coalition of Anti-Jackson Democrats, Anti-Masons, and National Republicans. The Whigs backed Noble and won their first gubernatorial victory. Noble's re-election was the first of three straight Whig victories in the Statehouse. The first-ever Democratic state convention, meanwhile, was held in 1834. The Democrats nominated James G. Read for governor. Voters in the three-county area that made up the original Clark's Grant went for Read. Scott County switched to Noble (it had backed Read in 1831), although by a slim thirteen-vote margin.[20]

The Whigs' success in southern Indiana was due primarily to the voters' hunger for an improved transportation system to move goods outside their immediate area. The Whig candidates promised a state initiative to fund internal improvements that swung normally Jacksonian-thinking residents away from Read. Even so, they continued their suspicion of East Coast financial interests and continued to support Jacksonian ideals on the national level. The Scott County vote for Noble was a turning point. Never before had its voters abandoned the Jeffersonian/Jacksonian-oriented candidate for governor, president, or Congress. It was the closest gubernatorial contest in the county to date. For the next thirty years, the county's voters exhibited a bifurcation that ultimately manifested itself in divergent views about temperance, fugitive slave laws, and the Civil War itself. The debates that turned brother against brother and husband against wife in the 1860s had their roots in the 1830s in Scott County.

The trend toward the Whig Party in Scott County continued in the mid-1830s as Democrats faced tougher races, and when victorious, survived with narrowing margins. In the 1835 congressional election, the incumbent Carr won his third term, this time over a Whig candidate, Charles Dewey, but Carr's margin in Scott County shrunk by 60 percent. In the 1836 legislative races, the first time party labels were attached to legislators, Scott County split, electing Democrat Samuel Heath as state representative, and Whig Isaac Hoagland, as state senator. Scott County even went narrowly for the Whig presidential candidate, William Henry Harrison, over Martin Van Buren. Because Harrison was considered a local hero, the presidential vote may be somewhat discounted, but the overall trend was confirmed when the county went for the second time in a row for the Whig candidate for governor in 1837, and switched from Democrat to Whig in its congressional choice, voting for the victor William Graham over John S. Simonson by about the same margin as they had voted for the Democrat Carr over the Whig Dewey in 1835.

The end of the 1830s produced some flip-flopping in Scott County political preferences. The state legislative delegation went Whig in 1838 (William Trulock for state representative), flipped to Democrat in 1839 (English for state representative and Carr for state senate), then back to Whig in 1840, with Aaron Rawlings as its state representative. Former congressman Carr reentered politics in 1839 to take back his seat for the Democrats, with Scott County providing a healthy margin.

A woodcut created for use on broadsides or banners during the Whigs' "log cabin" presidential campaign of 1840. In front of a log cabin, a shirt-sleeved William Henry Harrison welcomes a soldier, inviting him to rest and partake of a barrel of "Hard Cider."

The year 1840 brought better fortunes for Harrison. The Whig reversed his earlier defeat to Van Buren and took Scott County by virtually the same margin (thirty votes) as in 1836. Samuel Bigger, the Whig candidate for governor, made it three in a row for the Whigs in the Statehouse, with Scott County once again going Whig. The election of Harrison proved, however, to be a high-water mark for the Whig Party in Indiana. Scott County helped the third district throw Democrat Congressman Carr out of office in favor of the Whig, Joseph White, in the 1841 congressional election but he was the last Whig to represent the district.

In 1843 the Indiana congressional delegation again grew, this time to ten House members. Scott County once again became part of the second district, with more Democratic influence. The core of the old second and the third, Scott, Clark, and Jefferson Counties, remained together in the new second district.

For the next several years, Scott County displayed symptoms of political schizophrenia, in that its voters continued to vote for Whig congressional candidates in direct contradiction to the rest of the district, and, at the same time, shifted to elect a mostly Democratic legislative delegation. For example, Scott County turned against Democrat congressman Thomas Henley in 1845, voting instead for the losing Whig candidate, Roger Martin. In 1847 the county backed a Whig over Henley. This time it was John S. Davis. In 1849 the county favored the Whig, William McKee Dunn, over the Democrat victor, Cyrus Dunham. Commonsense would dictate that these Whig candidates would have been from Scott County, thus justifying the county's break for a Whig. However, none of the congressional candidates mentioned above, winners or losers, were from the county.

The state representative contests may have been most telling of Scott County residents' views on legislative issues because for many years the county had its own state representative. It shared a state senator with two neighboring counties. Beginning in 1842, Scott County sent English, a Democrat, back to the Indiana House, then shifted to David McClure, another Democrat, in 1843 and 1844. Democrat Sam Davis took the seat in 1845. Whigs briefly rebounded in Scott County in 1846 and 1847 when Horatio Holland and Doctor Alonzo Manson served single terms. Democrat Hezekiah Smith took the seat in 1848, and Manson was reelected in 1849.

Despite the continuous trading of the Indiana House seat between Democrats and Whigs, no incumbents were defeated and there were no rematches. It was almost as if people were taking turns offering themselves and serving. In most of the legislative elections the margin of victory for either party was less than 5 percent. Margins in legislative races can only be determined after 1843 because it was not until 1844 that county clerks were required to report election results to the secretary of state's office. Prior to 1844, a list of the winners, without vote totals or even the names of their opponents, was forwarded to the House and Senate clerks.

Governor Bigger retained Scott County's loyalty by three votes, in his 1843 re-election campaign, but he lost to Democrat James Whitcomb. The Bigger loss marked the end of a streak of Whig governors, and signaled a shift in sentiment among Hoosiers who bought into the Democrat philosophy of humanitarianism—the philosophy that society's obligation is to improve the condition of the human race across a broad spectrum. Throughout the 1830s Whigs were able to take credit for a growing economy and championed state bank charters, construction of the Michigan Road, the opening of streams and rivers to navigation, and the ill-fated canal system. They were able to blame the panic of 1837 on federal policies under President Van Buren.[21] But when things did not improve under President John Tyler (Harrison served one month), the Democrats were able to sell their slate of social issues.

At this time in Indiana, the insane were kept in jail with criminals. A third of adults were illiterate, and the number was growing. The blind and disabled were left to the mercy of relatives and friends. Governor Whitcomb promised and delivered much of the social services infrastructure that is still employed today in Indiana. Whitcomb's administration built the Blind School, established state institutions for the insane, and formalized the public school system.[22]

The year 1843 also marked the beginning of a two-election run for the Liberty Party in Indiana. The Liberty ticket never caught on in Scott County. Its candidate for governor scored one vote in the county in 1843 and zero votes in 1846. That year Scott County again backed the Whig candidate, Joseph G. Marshall, for governor, but Whitcomb was reelected and continued his program of social services improvements. As in gubernatorial politics, Scott County backed the Whig Clay in 1844 for president and gave one vote to the Liberty Party's James Birney.

The Mexican War sent shockwaves through Indiana politics when Zachary Taylor smeared Hoosier soldiers in his official report on the battle of Buena Vista. Taylor claimed the Hoosiers cut and ran when the battle became intense. The reaction in Indiana was swift. Indiana went for Lewis Cass for president in 1848 and newspapers across the state expressed indignation at Taylor's report. Scott County stuck with Taylor though, giving him a nine-vote margin over Cass. In just eight years, Van Buren's support in Scott County had dropped from 361 votes in 1840 to 16 votes in 1848. The former president had switched from the Democratic Party to the Free-Soil Party, which explains his diminishing popularity in Scott County.

The decade closed with another Democrat victory in the governor's race. Joseph Wright beat the Whig and Free-Soil candidates, with Scott County again backing the Whig, J. A. Matson. The Free-Soilers fared no better in Scott County than did the earlier Liberty Party. Free-Soiler James H. Cravens, not to be confused with Congressman James Cravens, received only five votes in Scott County. Van Buren's and Cravens's poor showings in Scott County reinforce the fact that Liberty/Free-Soil ideas never caught on in the county. They also document the ideological foundation that developed during this era that burst forth as the Copperhead movement more than a decade later.

As 1850 dawned Indiana was on the verge of its most volatile political decade. Prior to this point a staunchly Democrat state, the triple issues of Compromise, Kansas, and temperance were to split the state and the venerable Democrat Party at the seams. The political pendulum in Scott County, meanwhile, continued to swing, with deep-seated rifts appearing by the end of the decade.

Hoosiers in 1850 were generally looking forward to reaping the benefits of a growing population and an expanding economy. While the rate of immigration in southern Indiana had slowed, central and northern Indiana were quickly adding population, particularly in Marion, Saint Joseph, and Allen Counties. The inauguration of the east-west railroad service in the 1850s helped shift commerce away from the Ohio River and toward the state's interior. Indiana was becoming a boom state.

The great issue of the day, slavery, had not greatly impacted Indiana to date. By 1820 remnants of slavery had virtually disappeared,[23] although Abraham Kimberlin still owned a slave (Collins) as late as 1834. Hoosiers were generally tolerant of slavery in the South, and even those who were opposed to slavery in Indiana were more antiblack than they were antislavery or proslavery.[24] Indiana's collective attitude toward blacks was expressed through its active involvement in the colonization movement, a loose confederation of political leaders, church congregations, and businessmen across the North who favored encouraging free blacks to move to or colonize their ancestral continent of Africa. The Indiana Colonization Society formed in 1829, a full twelve years after the national organization began. It convinced the Indiana General Assembly to twice petition Congress for federal funds to promote colonization. The legislature also set up, but spent little, from a state colonization fund.[25]

Prominent Indiana colonization advocates included Indianapolis banker Calvin Fletcher, noted preacher Henry Ward Beecher, and Governor Joseph Wright, a Democrat. In 1850 the two dominant leaders of the majority Democrat Party, which controlled both houses of the general assembly and the governor's office, were Wright and his political nemesis, Jesse Bright of Madison. Wright was a Methodist, a populist, and an "Indiana first" man who believed in center-oriented policies that were most likely to keep harmony in his own party, and across party lines. He worked to keep Democrats from forming a northern Democratic Party, and tried to tamp out flames of sectionalism that arose from time to time. When Wright was asked to submit a representative motto from Indiana for inscription at the base of the Washington Monument, he wrote: "Indiana knows no North or South, nothing but the Union."[26]

Bright, eventually to become the most infamous U.S. Senator in Indiana history, was a states' rights Democrat who urged a conservative course for Indiana and the nation. He was a machine Democrat who relied on his control of patronage to rule the party. He could stack a convention as well as anyone.[27] Bright served on the Senate committee, chaired by Clay, that drafted the Compromise of 1850, a package of measures the most controversial of which was the Fugitive Slave Act. Newspapers across the state flung heated editorials at each other, and at the politicians who voted for the bill. Bright's vote on the Fugitive Slave Act is not recorded, but he voted for all other Compromise measures, and said, "I endorse it broadly, distinctly, and emphatically."[28] U.S. Senator James Whitcomb voted for the entire package, and Indiana's Democratic delegation in the U.S. House split on the bill. The only Whig member of the state's delegation voted for the Compromise. The *Madison Courier*, the dominant newspaper in Jefferson County and nearby counties including Scott, blasted the Compromise, calling it "repugnant to the feelings of a man living in a free state."[29] Most politicians, however, tried to declare the Compromise as producing an end to the "eternal agitation" on the slavery issue. The practical effect of the Compromise was to begin a split in the Democrat Party between men who had Free-Soil leanings and those who believed in either Bright's conservative approach or Wright's embrace of compromise. Whigs were similarly split, with compromisers peeling off to join the Democrats, and Free-Soilers looking for a home that fit their ideological comfort zone.

At the same time as the Compromise issue, Indiana drafted and debated a new constitution. Since the Democrat Party controlled the state in 1850, two-thirds of the delegates to the constitutional convention were Democrats. The resulting document reflected their political and social philosophies. Under the proposed constitution, noncitizens would be able to vote as long as they had been a resident of Indiana for one year and met other requirements. Also included, but voted on separately, was the infamous Article 13 that prohibited the immigration of African Americans into the state. In August 1851 both the constitution and Article 13 were overwhelmingly approved by voters, with only a few counties in northern and east central Indiana voting against Article 13. Scott County was almost unanimous in its approval of both: 784 for the constitution and 92 against; 913 for Article 13, and 66 against. More Scott County residents

U.S. Senator Jesse Bright from Indiana, 1859. After his tumultuous Hoosier political career, Bright served in the Kentucky legislature and later moved to Baltimore, dying there on May 20, 1875.

turned out to vote against African Americans than showed up to vote for their new constitution.[30]

The new constitution also altered the timing and frequency of state elections and the meetings of the general assembly. Upon ratification, state and local elections were to be conducted in October every other year, and the legislature was to meet every other year as well.[31] Annual elections for the Indiana House were ended, and the terms of governor and state senator were set at four years. The state and presidential elections would not be synchronized until 1881.

Two additional factors heightened the emotional turmoil about the Compromise: the publication of Harriet Beecher Stowe's *Uncle Tom's Cabin* in 1852, which touched off a reading frenzy akin to contemporary releases of a new *Harry Potter* volume, and the fugitive slave case of Indianapolis's John Freeman.[32] Freeman spent nine weeks in jail while authorities sorted out the claims of a Missouri man who said the African American businessman was actually his slave. Ultimately, Freeman's status as a free man was confirmed, but not before stirring up passions in Indiana once again.

During the election of 1852, both political parties tried again, this time successfully, to stamp the Compromise as final. Neither party campaigned on slavery issues. Also, the Whigs mounted a lackluster campaign. Wright was reelected governor by 10,000 votes.[33] Franklin Pierce was favored over the Whig, Winfield Scott, in the presidential race, and Democrats dominated legislative races. Ironically, Scott County rejected its state representative, William English, in his bid for Congress, choosing John Ferguson, the Whig, instead. Nevertheless, English won the race and went on to serve until 1861. There are no contemporary newspaper accounts to explain why English lost his home county after being Speaker of the House in his only term in the legislature. Without stretching the imagination too far, one could suggest that possibly his family's history of foreclosing on farm property in the county finally earned him enough enemies that he lost his hometown loyalties. As noted earlier, English never returned to live in Scott County after leaving an eight-year congressional career.

The elections in Scott County in October 1853 showed how local politics can really be. The Kimberlin family, whose civic profile had been limited to serving on grand juries, as road-district supervisors, and as election officials, pushed young Isaac Newton Kimberlin to victory in the county coroner's race. One of Isaac's opponents was his cousin, Philip Stark. In their home township of Lexington, where another cousin, Barnett Whitlach, was precinct inspector, Isaac outpolled Philip twelve votes to three. Isaac took the county by a mere two votes.[34] One might think that the victory in the coroner's race signaled that a Kimberlin had attained the lofty position of physician as well. Not so. Then, as now, one does not have to be a physician to serve as coroner in Indiana. Isaac gained greater notoriety ten years later for his bravery in front of the batteries of Vicksburg.

As the elected congressman from a district whose citizens were primarily of southern ancestry, English felt he had the popular support back home to advocate pro-southern policies in Congress. Known as the "slaveholder's ally,"[35] English quickly became embroiled in the weakening of the 1850 Compromise, ultimately symbolized by the Kansas-Nebraska debate. The issue at hand was whether the Kansas Territory should be admitted to the Union as a slave state or as a free state. Southern Democrats, who held the most powerful positions in Congress, favored admitting Kansas as a slave state. Most northern Democrats, led on this issue by Stephen Douglas of Illinois, favored a vote of the people on any constitution that dealt with the slavery issue. The philosophy espoused by Douglas became known as popular sovereignty.

English was a member of the House Committee on Territories, and he used that platform to push for popular sovereignty in territories where

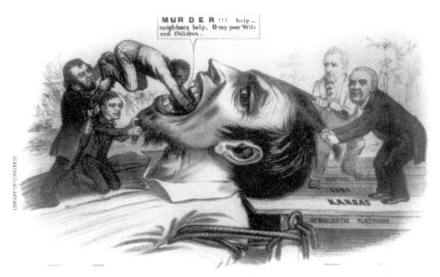

A cartoonist gives the Democratic Party the major blame for violence perpetrated against antislavery settlers in Kansas in the wake of the Kansas-Nebraska Act. A bearded "freesoiler" has been bound to the Democratic platform and is restrained by two Lilliputian figures, presidential nominee James Buchanan and Democratic senator Lewis Cass. Democratic senator Stephen A. Douglas and president Franklin Pierce, also shown as tiny figures, force a black man into the giant's gaping mouth.

the question of slaveholding hung in the balance. In a speech before Congress on May 9, 1853, English said that "the great mass of the North will stand firm by the side of their southern brethren in support of the principles of nonintervention and of popular sovereignty."[36]

Douglas's sponsorship of the Kansas-Nebraska Act was an attempt to bring an end to the debate. The act nullified the Missouri Compromise of 1820 and replaced it with popular sovereignty.[37] English voted for the Kansas-Nebraska Act on March 30, 1854. Passage of the act ultimately helped ignite the ensuing bloodshed ("Bleeding Kansas") that involved rival factions of proslavery forces infiltrating from Missouri, and antislavery forces coming from other northern states. Proslavery forces in Kansas concentrated around LeCompton seized control of the territorial legislature and passed a law legalizing slavery. They wrote a proslavery constitution and applied for admission to the Union as a new state. The antislavery forces rallied in Topeka and elected their own governor and legislature.[38]

As intense as debate among Hoosiers over Kansas-Nebraska was, discussions about temperance was even livelier. The *Madison Courier* predicted that temperance would overshadow all other issues in the 1854 election.[39] A temperance convention early that year drew people of all political persuasions, who resolved that confiscation and destruction of all liquor was necessary. The Democrats, in their convention, rejected the fanaticism of the temperance movement, opting instead for statements about the evils of alcohol. The half-hearted Democratic stance drove even more people away from the Democrat Party than the controversial Kansas-Nebraska Act did, for different reasons.

Also in 1854 opposing sides of the immigration issue became active. In 1850 there were 55,000 foreign-born people in Indiana. By 1860 there were 120,000 nonnatives. Most of these were Irish or German, and most were Democrats.[40] Recognizing the Democrat leanings of the immigrants, the delegates to the 1850 constitutional convention removed citizenship as a requisite for voting. In reaction, the Know Nothing Party, a nativist group with roots in anti-immigrant sentiment, became very active in Indiana.[41]

Their own party floundering after the Kansas-Nebraska Act, many Whigs flocked to the Know Nothings, as did conservative Democrats. Meanwhile Free-Soil Democrats became Free Democrats, while those Democrats and Whigs who favored restoration of the Missouri Compromise held a fusion convention in July 1854, eight weeks after the disastrous Democratic convention, and formed the People's Party. The new party elected its entire 1854 state ticket, along with nine of eleven congressional seats, and took control of the Indiana House.[42]

The Know Nothing Party, not strong enough in Indiana to run its own slate of statewide candidates, decided to hijack the People's Party convention in Indianapolis. The Know Nothings succeeded in electing their own party members to three-fourths of the delegate positions in the People's Party convention. They were given credit by newspapers throughout the state for the sweeping People's Party victory from congressional to local races.[43]

LIBRARY OF CONGRESS

An antislavery Democrat, Oliver P. Morton moved to the People's Party and eventually the Republican Party, becoming Indiana's first native-born governor in 1861.

Temperance did in fact overshadow Kansas-Nebraska in the legislative races. The Democrats were able to hold on to the Senate,[44] but only the far south of Indiana remained solidly in the Democrat ranks, with William English of Lexington (the Kimberlin family seat) and Seth Miller keeping their congressional seats.

In addition to the split in the Democratic Party, two residual impacts occurred. Schuyler Colfax rode the People's Party ticket to victory in a congressional race in South Bend, and the U.S. Senate seat sat vacant until 1857 because the divided Indiana legislature could not agree on a candidate. Bright was the sole U.S. Senator from Indiana for three years, which caused his influence over patronage and his party's machinery to grow beyond even his outsized proportions. Temperance faded as an issue in 1855 in spite of the passage by the general assembly of a strong temperance law. Later that year, the Indiana Supreme Court declared prohibition unconstitutional, ruling that banning the use of one's property (for example, grain to make alcohol) was an improper taking of that property's value.

By 1856 the Republican Party had gained strength in Indiana, even though it would be two years before Indiana candidates ran under its

A lithograph depicting the May 22, 1856, attack and severe beating of Massachusetts senator Charles Sumner by Representative Preston S. Brooks of South Carolina. Brooks's fellow South Carolinian representative, Lawrence M. Keitt, stands in the center, raising his own cane menacingly to stay possible intervention by the other legislators.

banner. Delegates to the People's Party convention agreed to send delegates to the Republican Party National Convention as well. In Indiana the People's Party tried to steer a course between opposition to the Kansas-Nebraska Act and outright abolitionism. The party nominated candidates such as Oliver Morton of Centerville, who was seen by some, such as George Julian, to be simply an opportunist.[45] In reality, Morton was a former Democrat who had supported the Compromise of 1850 and rejected Free-Soiler tendencies. By the end of 1854, however, he was campaigning against the Kansas-Nebraska Act and for the People's Party.

The Know Nothing Party was less relevant and less effective in 1856. The party nominated Millard Fillmore for president, but during the course of the year faded until its principal strength was in extreme southern Indiana. Bright announced himself a candidate for president, but his campaign was short-lived. When he realized his support lay only in Indiana, and even at that, only in southern Indiana, he threw his support to James Buchanan's candidacy.[46]

Without any overriding state issues to debate, the 1856 campaign focused on the violence in Kansas. Hoosiers were drawn into the debate by those who had immigrated to, or visited, Kansas. During the continuing battle over the future of the Kansas Territory, English consistently promoted the proslavery cause. When House colleague Preston Brooks of South Carolina caned U.S. Senator Charles Sumner of Massachusetts for remarks made on the Senate floor, English voted against expelling Brooks from Congress. Calvin Fletcher and Ovid Butler, among others, formed a committee to raise a militia to go fight in Kansas. Violence broke out between Republicans and Know Nothings in Clark County, Indiana. Democrats tried to ally with the Know Nothings in Clark and Scott Counties. They accused Republicans of being "amalgamationists" and paraded white girls carrying banners that read, "Fathers, save us from nigger husbands."[47]

The central issue of the campaign was summed up well by the *Indianapolis Sentinel*, a pro-Democrat organ of the state's most powerful politician, Bright, when it said: "Black Republicans are for full citizenship for the Negro. The Democracy opposes it."[48] Buchanan's pledge to seek peace between proslavery and antislavery sections of the country and his support for popular sovereignty allowed him to gain the presidency, with 45 percent of the popular vote. His appointee for territorial governor, John Geary, was able to restore peace in Kansas, at least temporarily.

Buchanan defeated Charles Fremont by 26,000 votes in Indiana. The Democratic gubernatorial nominee, Ashbel Willard of Evansville, defeated Morton of the People's Party by 5,800 votes. Morton lost Scott and Clark Counties, but won in Jefferson County by nearly 500 votes. His victory in Jefferson County is not surprising given that the *Madison Courier* had strenuously opposed the Kansas-Nebraska Act and had continued to give wide coverage to acts of violence in the territories. English faced difficulty in his re-election effort in Indiana because of the vehemence of his pro-slavery stance. "Black Republicans" hung English in effigy and added him to the "roll of infamy" for his Kansas-Nebraska vote. English survived. In fact, he was one of only three northern members of the U.S. House who survived the 1856 election after voting for the Kansas-Nebraska Act. The second congressional district, which included Scott and Clark Counties (Jefferson County had been redistricted into the third after the 1850 census.) reelected English by 2,600 votes over the People's Party candidate, John Wilson. The parties split the legislature, with the Democrats retaking the House, and the People's Party taking the Senate. The Democratic Party had rebounded for now.

When the LeCompton constitutional convention convened in Kansas Territory in 1857 under alleged fraudulent circumstances (fifteen counties had no delegates, and antislavery forces refused to participate),[49] delegates "incorporated nearly the whole of Kentucky and Missouri's slave codes" into the document (Article 7).[50] But the greatest debate was about whether to submit the draft constitution to territorial voters for ratification. President Buchanan had come out in favor of submission, but the convention in the end voted to submit only Article 7 to the voters. Even that compromise was deemed fraudulent. The ballot language provided that if the LeCompton Constitution was rejected, slave property was still to be protected.[51] The large antislavery majority of territorial voters therefore boycotted the vote altogether. The LeCompton Constituion was approved by the proslavery settlers who voted on December 21, 1857.

Rather than feeling chastised by his close re-election campaign, English grew bolder when he returned to Congress. When Congress took up the LeCompton Constitution, he positioned himself as a proslavery member who was opposed to the constitution because it had not been submitted in whole to the voters. On April 1, 1858, the House voted 120 to 112 to send the LeCompton Constitution back for ratification by voters in Kansas. The U.S. Senate rejected the idea and a conference committee was formed. English was one of three House members of the conference committee (along with Alexander Stephens, a Democrat from Georgia, and William Howard, an Opposition Party member from Michigan). The Opposition Party had formed for the 1854 elections as a home to former Whigs who were opposed to the Democrats, but not comfortable with the Know Nothings (the Republican Party did not form until 1856). After the 1854 congressional elections, the Opposition Party was actually the majority party in Congress, with one hundred members. The party, however, did not control the flow of legislation, because the Speaker of the House, Nathaniel Prentice Banks, was a compromise speaker. Banks was a former Democrat who ran as a Know Nothing in 1854 and as a Republican in 1856.

Despite pledging to his constituents that he would not vote for the LeCompton Constitution for Kansas, English led the maneuvering for its ratification on the conference committee. He agreed to ally with Stephens to protect Buchanan's interests by forming an indirect ratification requirement for the LeCompton Constitution.[52] The English bill required Kansas voters to choose between a reduced land grant of four million acres with the constitution and slavery, or to reject the smaller land grant. This way, voters would seemingly be voting on the land grant and slavery would be a secondary issue.[53] Senator Douglas broke with Buchanan and spoke out against English's legislation. Despite his opposition, the "English Swindle," as it became known, passed Congress on April 30, 1858, by a vote of 112 to 103 in the House and 31 to 22 in the Senate. On August 2, 1858, the voters of Kansas Territory overwhelmingly rejected the ballot question, with 11,300 opposed, and 1,788 in favor. Kansas would have to wait until it reached a population of 90,000 inhabitants to try again for statehood.

The aftermath of the Kansas vote was quickly felt in Indiana. Republicans picked up three congressional seats and took control of both houses of the legislature. English was reelected once again, however, claiming that he gave Hoosiers and Kansans what they wanted, a chance to vote on the LeCompton Constitution. English continued to sympathize with the South throughout the remaining years of the Buchanan administration. As the North and South grew farther apart and talk of secession became amplified at the close of the 1850s, English gave what is considered his most memorable speech in Congress, begging the South to stay within the Union, but holding himself up as their staunch ally at the same time. Portions of the January 3, 1860 speech read like something John Calhoun would say rather than a northern Hoosier. English declared "we are determined to stand by you [the South] and to join you in a war of political extermination against your foes." Later in that same speech, English implored, "We can win at the ballot box or muster more men with the cartridge box, too, if it becomes necessary to resort to these to defend your constitutional rights of a confederacy."[54]

English's mind was on pursuits other than politics as the watershed year of 1860 dawned. He began negotiations to purchase the Jeffersonville branch of the Third State Bank of Indiana, owned by Hugh McCulloch, future U.S. Secretary of the Treasury under Presidents Abraham Lincoln, Andrew Johnson, and Chester Arthur.[55] Historian F. Gerald Handfield Jr. noted that "more important non-political opportunities beckoned the ever-ambitious English, now 38 years old, and wise to connections between business and politics."[56] English chose not to stand for re-election that year, choosing instead to return to Indiana to look after his business interests. He moved to Indianapolis, where he co-founded the First National Bank of Indianapolis in 1863, with $150,000 in start-up capital contributed by James Lanier, George Riggs, and eight others, including Indianapolis newspaper editor John New.[57] English continued his active involvement in the Democratic Party by serving as State Democrat Chair from 1866 to 1869, and eventually running unsuccessfully for vice president on the Winfield Hancock ticket in 1880. Summing up his career late in life, English told an interviewer, "I was a business machine."[58]

The delicate balance between Democrat strength and People's/Republican Party momentum in Indiana continued through 1857 and 1858. The LeCompton Constitution, which gave proslavery forces in Kansas the upper hand in determining the future of Kansas as a state, caused a new split in the Democrat Party. Indiana's congressional delegation favored it and Kansas's admission to the Union under the "LeComptonites." In contrast, Democrat newspapers generally editorialized against the LeCompton Constitution as a violation of popular sovereignty. Bright was branded a "tool of the South"[59] for his unflinching support of Buchanan and his support of the LeCompton Constitution. This was the beginning of Bright being identified as a southern sympathizer, which would get him in big trouble four years later.

It was a little known move by Governor Willard, however, that had the most far-reaching impact on Indiana in the coming years. In 1857 Willard borrowed money to pay interest on state bonds when partisanship in the general assembly caused the proper appropriation not to be passed. Morton would cite this incident as precedent when he kept the state treasury afloat during the Civil War with money borrowed outside legal channels. Also, in October 1857, the People's Party officially took the Republican Party name in Indiana. The Republicans captured the same congressional seats as the People's Party had two years before. The Democrats swept the state ticket, while the Republicans took the House from the Democrats and kept hold of the Senate majority inherited from the People's Party.

As the decade ended, Scott County stood among the preeminent counties in Indiana, exerting political power well beyond the size of its population may have justified. The county could boast that it was the birthplace and nurturing ground for one of Indiana's three most influential Democrats—English, Bright, and Wright. In its first forty years the county had developed a solid political tradition founded upon the principles of the Jacksonian democracy and the conservative southern social mores that were manifest in its citizens. Its officeholders, indeed those of the entire second congressional district in the persons of Bright and English, took those values to Indianapolis and to Washington, D.C., where they were important players in holding southern Indiana close in heart and in policy to their Southern brethren. Bright and English each reached their political zenith in the 1850s and both would be out of office by 1861. Their legacy, however, cast its shadow across Indiana politics during the dark years of the coming Civil War. Politicians such as second district Congressman James A. Cravens took up their mantle and helped give rise to the name "Copperhead" for which Scott County and its neighbors would forever be known.

4

Fighting and Dying for the Union

Indiana in 1860 presented a significantly different political land-
scape than had been the case ten years earlier. In 1850 the Democrats
had been consolidating gains made at the expense of the disintegrating
Whig Party. The Republican Party was now on the verge of scoring similar
victories over a tired and split Democrat Party. Indiana Whigs had finally
accepted the Republican ascendancy; and in an attempt to keep them in
line, the former People's Party candidate for governor, Oliver Morton,
suggested downplaying the slavery issue and nominating former Whig
Henry Lane for governor. The payoff for Morton was that if Republicans
won both houses of the legislature, Lane would immediately be elected
U.S. Senator, and Morton would walk into the governor's office without a
fight.[1] The deal worked, but the attempt to downplay the slavery issue did
not. Debates over slavery ignited all over the state.

Each party tried to portray the other as "Negro loving." The Democrats
said the Republicans preferred African Americans to white foreigners and
were prepared to import hordes of free blacks into Indiana to compete
with white labor. The Republicans claimed that it was the Democrats
who would spread slavery to the territories and thus prevent the children
of Hoosiers from seeking their fortunes in the West. The fact was that
neither party favored equality for African Americans. Candidates fought
over fine gradations of how the Fugitive Slave Act should be enforced,
for example. Hoosier delegates to the Republican National Convention
favored Abraham Lincoln over William Seward, the former New York
governor and U.S. Senator, because they thought Lincoln was less of an
antislavery candidate than Seward.

One of the key constituencies to be fought for was the immigrant vote. As stated earlier, the foreign-born population of Indiana had more than doubled in ten years. Most of these were Irish and Germans who were traditionally Democrats. The Republican Party sent German-speaking campaigners, including Carl Schurz, John Popp, and Charles Coulon, into Indiana and published thousands of election flyers in German. In the end, these efforts were heralded by newspapers as contributing heavily to Lincoln's narrow victory in Indiana. It was not until 1967, when Thomas Kelso took the time to analyze actual election returns from nine Indiana counties with German-dominated townships, that historians were finally able to say with finality: "Traditional theses about a Republican voting pattern among Germans is not supported by data from Indiana."[2] Kelso determined that the "Germans did not overlook those aspects within the new party which were presumed to be anti-immigrant,"[3] including: the Republican Party's Know-Nothing roots, a temperance element within the party that was anathema to Germans, and the party's image as being more problack equality than for equal rights for immigrants.[4] Kelso traced the erroneous assumption of a "glorious German contribution to Lincoln's victory," to books written at the beginning of the twentieth century by German historians Julius Goebbel (1904), Georg Von Bosse (1908), and A. B. Faust (1909).[5]

In the race for Indiana governor, Lane defeated former congressman Thomas Hendricks by nearly 10,000 votes.[6] Scott County went for Hendricks, as did Clark County, while Jefferson County held true to its past and favored Lane by more than 800 votes.[7] A new face won the second congressional district seat. Democrat James A. Cravens of Washington County defeated Republican John Davies by a narrow margin of 539 votes.[8] Cravens lost Floyd and Perry Counties along the Ohio River, but he took both Scott and Clark Counties. Cravens played a prominent role in Civil War politics in southern Indiana as he tried to ride the fence between his Union and Copperhead constituents.

The year 1861 arrived with one state, South Carolina, already seceded from the Union. While Democrats had warned during the past campaign that a Republican victory would bring about Civil War, both parties tried to find ways to preserve the Union in the winter of 1861. Union meetings were held across the state with members of both parties attending. The *Madison Courier* called for a joint meeting of the Kentucky and Indiana legislatures to try to mitigate the crisis. Compromise, generally in the

A veteran of the Mexican-American war, James A. Cravens of Indiana served in Congress from 1861 to 1865. He died in Hardinsburg, Indiana, on June 20, 1893.

form of stricter adherence to the Fugitive Slave Act for the sake of Union, was promoted particularly in southern Indiana, where ties to the South were closest. Rallies and county conventions were held in virtually every Ohio River county, and many, such as Perry County, declared that its true interests lay with the South. Economic and kinship ties made the sentiments, and even loyalty, of many southern Hoosiers suspect throughout the war to come.

Demagogues and Disunion

The most bizarre Civil War-era drama involving southern Indiana politicians was the ouster of Jesse Bright from the U.S. Senate. Bright was a resident of Madison, a confidant of William English, and a backer of John C. Breckinridge over Stephen Douglas for the 1860 Democratic presidential nomination. Bright had earlier served as a member of the Common Council (First Ward) of Madison, as a state senator from 1841 to 1843, and as lieutenant governor from 1843 to 1845 before his election to the U.S. Senate by the general assembly in 1845.[9] It was his support of Breckinridge that got him in trouble with his own state party. The Democrats rejected Bright's chosen slate of candidates in the 1860 state convention[10] and went with a broader Douglas slate. Even in Indiana, where Bright and English were prominent supporters of Breckinridge, local Democrats shifted to Douglas.[11] Breckenridge received only 12,300 votes in Indiana, compared to 115,500 for Douglas.[12]

Bright's correspondence with Jefferson Davis during the secession crisis fatally damaged his relationships in the Senate. Bright addressed a letter, dated March 1, 1861, to "Jefferson Davis, President of the Confederate States," and suggested to his old friend the name of an arms dealer who offered fair prices. When the Senate erupted in protest at Bright's implicit recognition of the Confederacy, Bright wrote to English, "There is some talk, I understand, of their expelling me on account of my known disloyalty. Let it come, I have got so that I believe nothing I read and am not surprised at anything that takes place."[13] Bright is the last U.S. Senator in history to be expelled from that body. After his expulsion in February 1862, Bright moved to Kentucky, served two terms in the legislature there from 1867 to 1871, and died in 1875.

Equally resistant to compromise was the new Indiana governor, Morton, who traveled to Washington, D.C., in March 1861 to offer Lincoln 6,000 Hoosier troops to help in putting down the imminent rebellion. In a speech celebrating Lincoln's victory, Morton had said, "If it was worth a bloody struggle to form the nation, it is worth one to preserve it."[14] Even before the shelling of Fort Sumter, some prominent Democrats began to move away from mainstream Hoosier thinking. While most citizens were still struggling with their feelings about the Confederacy, Congress-

U.S. Senator Daniel Voorhees of Terre Haute, Indiana

man Daniel Voorhees, elected in 1860 and known as the Tall Sycamore of the Wabash, acted as an early counterpoint to Morton. At a meeting in Greencastle on April 10, 1861, Voorhees blasted away at talk of calling up troops. "Not one dollar and not one man from Indiana with which to subjugate the South and inaugurate Civil War," he said.[15] Voorhees did not have to worry about an invasion by the North. Two days later, Fort Sumter, commanded by Hoosier major Robert Anderson, was shelled into submission. And the Civil War was on.

Voorhees became one of the prominent national leaders of the "Peace Democrat" movement. Along with Clement Vallandigham of Ohio and others, Voorhees tried throughout the war to maneuver Union military and political commanders, including Lincoln, to the negotiating table. Voorhees believed that Lincoln had no right to use force to preserve the Union, and that only economic self-interest could entice the South back into the fold.

A Confederate flag flies over the ruins of Fort Sumter. Although rebels occupied the fort, they withstood an almost constant bombardment by federal forces from July 1863 to February 1865.

At least one of Voorhees's Democratic colleagues was willing to go further. Second district Congressman James Cravens, in a letter to English dated three days before the fall of Fort Sumter, proposed that the southern portions of Indiana, Ohio, and Illinois be separated into a new state called Jackson and that this new state would secede.[16] "I cannot obliviate [*sic*] the fact that our interest is with the South and I cannot reconcile the separation, and it will be the last day in the evening before I consent to fight them," wrote Cravens.[17]

According to historian Emma Lou Thornbrough, "Sumter had an electrifying effect on Indiana."[18] Morton raised 12,000 troops within two weeks.[19] Heretofore "compromise" newspapers such as the *New Albany Ledger* and the *Indianapolis Sentinel* pledged support for the war. The *Sentinel*'s editor, J. J. Bingham, had a slight nudge along the path. Shortly after Sumter, a mob arrived at his home and forced him to go the mayor's office to swear loyalty to the Union.[20] The Indiana General Assembly became symbolic of the debate statewide. Republicans tried to corner the market on loyalty, embittering the Democrats who went out of their way to prove their patriotism. State Senator Smith Jones of Bartholomew County, in a letter to his friend Allen Hamilton, said, "There are no traitors in Indiana."[21]

Still, speeches such as that of State Representative Horace Heffren gave the suspicious plenty to talk about. During the 1861 legislative session, Heffren, who represented Washington and Harrison Counties, said he would "gladly bear the epithet '*traitor*'" because he sympathized with the South. Heffren claimed more than 100,000 Hoosiers stood ready to prevent any Indiana army "under abolition banners" from crossing the Ohio River. When asked if he would fight against the Union, he said, "I will leave my native land, my hearthstone, my wife and family and become a private in the southern army, rather than be the commander-in-chief of an abolition army."[22] Heffren later did a flip-flop, accepting a commission as a lieutenant colonel in the Fiftieth Indiana Volunteer Infantry Regiment, and then resigning his commission to join the Sons of Liberty (an anti-Morton group whose membership and mission are murky, at best).[23]

Defeat, Draft, and Emancipation

With southern Indiana politicians fanning the flames, 1862 did not promise to be a good year for the Union cause in Indiana. Benjamin Kimberlin sounded hopeful in a letter to his brother, Jacob R., while in reserve before Corinth, Mississippi. Benjamin wrote:

> the other great battle that has long been expected here has not come off yet, but we are almost expecting it to commence every day our pickets and the rebel pickets has a skirmish nearly every day and I think there cant be many days before a general engagement will take place for our army is advancing on Corinth slowly. Jake I don't know how it looks to you but I think the Secesh is nearly played out and if we whip them here it will bring the war nearly to a close. . . . let me know how all of your crop looks and how you are getting along generally particularly among the girls. As to the crop part I expect you are doing very well, for you wrote that you had a good plough team and was going to ploughing in a few days for corn, Jake I don't mean that you can get along better with a crop than you can with the girls for I think you are the boy that can get along very well with boath, not using any flattery or anything of the kind.[24]

Despite Benjamin's optimistic outlook, General George McClellan's failure to secure the Virginia Peninsula, Union defeat at Second Bull Run and in the Shenandoah Valley, and indecisive battles at Shiloh, Fair Oaks, and Antietam left Hoosiers doubting more than ever the wisdom of prolonging the war.

In June 1862 Congress authorized the states to implement a draft to meet their troop quota.[25] An enrollment officer was named for each county, with a deputy in each precinct. Any white male age eighteen to forty-five was eligible. The draft convinced thousands more Hoosiers, including a second wave of Kimberlins, to volunteer so they could choose their regiment. Between July 31 and August 11, a Lieutenant Campbell enrolled ten more members of the Kimberlin clan at Lexington. All ten signed up for Company K, Sixty-sixth Indiana Volunteers.[26] The entire Sixty-Sixth Indiana came from the second congressional district.[27] Like the Kimberlins in the Twenty-Third Indiana, the volunteers were treated to the sight of a prominent general when they arrived at Camp Noble to muster in. General Lew Wallace, former commander of the Twenty-Third, swore them in and gave them a pep talk.[28]

Daniel Kimberlin, at age thirty, was the oldest of the tight-knit group that became soldiers together on August 19, 1862. The five foot, nine inch grey-eyed redhead left for Lexington, Kentucky, the same day. Colonel Roger Martin planned to train the Sixty-Sixth at Camp Nelson

General Charles Cruft of Terre Haute, Indiana

near Nicholasville, but when they arrived, there was no time to play war. Confederate general Kirby Smith was reported moving north toward Richmond, Kentucky. On August 23 General William "Bull" Nelson sent the Sixty-sixth forty miles southeast of Lexington to the foot of Big Hill. There, on August 30, just south of Richmond, 6,500 Union soldiers under General Charles Cruft faced 16,000 Rebels.[29]

The battle consisted of three phases. During phase one, Manson's brigade took the brunt of General Patrick Cleburne's Rebel advance up the Richmond Road (US 421). While the Sixty-sixth Indiana was held in reserve as part of Cruft's brigade, Manson mistook Rebel skirmishers for the main Confederate advance and shifted his command east to counter it. Confederate general Thomas Churchill then brought his brigade through a draw to the west and outflanked Manson's right, forcing an orderly Union retreat.[30] Nelson ordered Cruft's brigade, including the Sixty-sixth, forward to Rogersville, where they set up a rallying point for Manson's command and established a defensive line across the Richmond Road. The Sixty-sixth tried three times to stop Rebel advances during a day when temperatures reached 100 degrees. They constantly fought and retreated, once making a desperate lunge across a hayfield at the Fourteenth and Tenth Texas Regiments at midday.[31]

The Sixty-sixth made its last stand along the south iron fence of the Richmond Cemetery, and then covered the general Union retreat through the center of Richmond.[32] At the end of the day, the Sixty-sixth was overwhelmed, and all of its members were either killed, wounded, or captured. While not an official surrender, the practical effect was that for nearly a year the unit was lost to the Union service.[33] Confederate casualties were 78 killed and 372 wounded. Union losses were 2,000 taken prisoner, 844 wounded, and 206 killed.[34] Daniel was one of those who perished. He

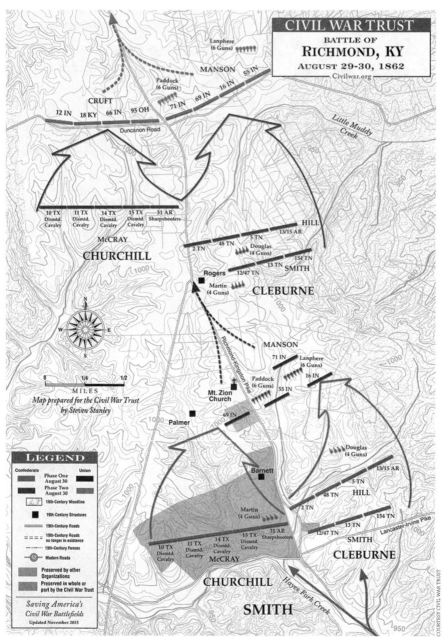

Map depicting the movement of Union and Confederate armies at the Battle of Richmond in Kentucky, August 29–30, 1862.

had been a soldier for just eleven days. The other nine Kimberlins and Whitlach cousins were paroled and spent the early fall in a parole camp in Indianapolis until they were released in the late fall. All nine rejoined their unit. The Kimberlin who had been designated a year earlier to stay behind on the farm finally volunteered when the draft began. Twenty-year-old Jacob "R.," the boy who had been the recipient of most of the letters from the battlefield to date, joined the Fifty-fourth Indiana for a three-month stint. Jacob wrote to old Isaac Jones Kimberlin from Russellville, Kentucky, on July 30, 1862: "It seems like I aught to be at home at work but if no bad luck should happen it wont be very long until I will . . . if that corn is not plowed at Henrys just let it a lone"[35]

Old Isaac replied on August 22 with all the news from Lexington:

The war Spirit runs high here a great number has lately volenteerd I will name some of them to wit Abraham Kimberlin, John S. Whitlatch, Reace and Alexander Whitlach, John, James and Daniel Varble, Daniel Kimberlin [he died at Richmond eight days later] William Hough and a great number about Lexington all went in the 66th Regt of Ind Vol there now somewhere in Ky. . . by what I see in the papers the rebels is deturmind to try Ky and Tenn again but I hope the good Lord will disappoint them in their wickedness . . . your affectionate Father even till Death.[36]

The dutiful son wrote from Bowling, Kentucky, on September 4, that he had made the right choice: "If I had staid at home I would been in the three years service now . . . I know you have a pretty hard time but take as good care of the things as you can a few days longer and I think I will be there."[37]

The most wrenching events of 1862 did not take place on the battlefield. Lincoln's dual announcements in September of his Emancipation Proclamation and the suspension of habeas corpus for those charged with disloyal acts[38] did more to stir up emotions in Indiana than any military defeat could have accomplished. The Democratic *Indianapolis Sentinel* editorialized that the Proclamation was "a blunder fraught with evil."[39] From the Proclamation forward, the justification for the war changed from preserving the Union to freeing the slaves. The Democratic slogan "The Constitution as it is, the Union as it was" was directly challenged.[40] War Democrats who had been known for being willing to fight to preserve

President Abraham Lincoln reads the Emancipation Proclamation to his cabinet. From left to right: Edwin M. Stanton, Secretary of War; Salmon P. Chase, Secretary of the Treasury; Lincoln; Gideon Welles, Secretary of the Navy; Caleb B. Smith, Secretary of the Interior; William H. Seward, Secretary of State; Montgomery Blair, Postmaster General; and Edward Bates, Attorney General.

the Union fled the Union Party that Morton had tried to hold together. Any sense of unity disappeared as the last thread connecting pro-Union Democrats and pro-Union Republicans wore through. It became more difficult for many Hoosiers to fight for what they now perceived as a war for African Americans.

Secret Societies

Morton recognized the danger to himself and the Union Party cause if the Copperheads were left unrestrained. He seized on careless statements by his political rivals Hendricks of Madison, Voorhees from Terre Haute; and Vallandigham of Ohio who all hinted at the possibility of a great "Northwest Confederacy," which would be separate from but allied with the South.

Morton used the *Indianapolis Journal* to proclaim the existence of "secret societies" whose mission was to subvert civil government in Indiana and to establish the Northwest Confederacy. A federal grand jury of fourteen Republicans actually investigated and indicted forty-seven Hoosiers in August 1862 on counts of treason and conspiracy. The *Journal* said on August 4 that "so gigantic a conspiracy is second only to the rebellion of which it is an offshoot."[41] No trials were held, but the indictments served Morton's purpose. Speculation about the existence of secret societies permeated public debates and affected public policy, individual careers, and personal lives throughout the war.

Historians disagree on whether the secret societies existed, and if so to what extent. In 1918 Indiana historian Mayo Fesler published the first attempt to document the existence of three groups that he claimed were formed independently, but had similar goals and some duplicative membership. According to Fesler, the Knights of the Golden Circle was formed in 1853 by Doctor George Bickley, a Cincinnati surgeon, in order to promote the colonization of Mexico.[42] The KGC evolved into an anti-Union society after its first convention in Raleigh, North Carolina, in 1860, and, according to Orange County, Indiana, tradition was brought to the Hoosier State by William Bowles, a Scott County native who settled in Paoli.[43] In an undated letter to his wife, Bowles wrote: "If Ky had gone out at the proper time, southern Ind. Would have been with her today, if

THE COPPERHEAD PARTY.——IN FAVOR OF *A VIGOROUS PROSECUTION OF PEACE!*

A February 28, 1863, editorial cartoon shows three caricatured Copperheads advancing on Columbia, who holds a shield labeled "Union" and a sword.

not the whole state."[44] Bowles may have been accurate in his assessment. His hometown newspaper, the *Paoli Eagle*, said that "in case of dissolution, Indiana's interest points to the South as the natural place for her to go."[45] The citizens of Perry County along the Ohio River voted in 1861 that if war should come, the dividing line should run not along the Ohio River, but north of the Perry County line.[46]

The wave of arrests that followed the suspension of habeas corpus, and General Ambrose Burnside's (a native of Liberty, Indiana) General Order Number 38 in April 1863, suppressed KGC activity to the point where it ceased to exist as an organization. General Order Number 38 said that anyone who "declared sympathy" for the enemy would be subject to military justice.[47]

A second group, the Order of the American Knights (founded in Missouri in 1863), according to Fesler, absorbed the mission of the KGC, but was never very strong in Indiana. The third organization, the Sons of Liberty, Fesler said, formed in Indiana in 1864 with Harrison Dodd, publisher of the Indianapolis City Directory, as state commander.[48] Fesler cited as evidence for the existence of these secret societies a series of incidents, some violent, that occurred across Indiana. These included the murder of a soldier on leave in French Lick, the murder of a grand jury witness in Morgan County, a shootout between KGC members and former legislator Louis Prosser in Brown County, and the organization and drilling of armed bands in Nashville's town square.[49]

Federal agents raided Voorhees's Terre Haute office in August 1863 and confiscated KGC literature and letters from former U.S. Senator James Walter Wall of New Jersey that told of the availability of 30,000 Garibaldi rifles.[50] A month earlier, in New Albany, agents arrested George Bickley, the KGC founder, as he tried to sneak the group's literature into Indiana.[51]

Fesler estimated the Indiana membership of the KGC to be 125,000, while the SOL membership was around 50,000.[52] The Indianapolis office of SOL Grand Commander Dodd was raided by a federal provost marshal looking for smuggled weapons. Discovered in the office were more than 350 navy revolvers and 135,000 rounds of ammunition.[53] The ultimate proof, according to Fesler, may have been the Battle of Pogue's Run in Indianapolis, on May 20, 1863. Fesler said that 3,000 armed "radicals" used the cover of a Democratic Party rally to plot the seizure of Camp Morton, a large prisoner of war camp, near present-day Twenty-second Street and Central

Avenue. Federal troops disrupted the rally and afterward stopped trains leaving town. According to Fesler, they confiscated about 500 guns.[54]

Writing in 1960, Frank Klement said the secret societies were "a political apparition. . . . It was a figment of Republican imagination . . . a contribution to American mythology."[55] In a sequel to his first work, Klement said the KGC was based, in part, on lies composed by Colonel Henry Carrington.[56] Carrington was a friend of Morton who owed his position as commander of the District of Indiana to Morton's intercession with General Burnside. According to Klement, Carrington "concocted an assortment of cock-and-bull stories, and related them to Burnside with a straight face"[57] Klement said that no lists of paid KGC or SOL membership were ever found and not a single chapter or "castle" existed in Indiana. Klement said Fesler did not turn up a single old-timer who admitted belonging to a secret society.[58]

A third historian, Lorna Lutes Sylvester, takes a position between Fesler and Klement. Sylvester said "claims by recent historians that Morton fabricated the entire KGC legend are questionable. To believe that endows Morton with an omnipotence that his most ardent admirers did not claim for him."[59] If, as some historians claimed, most Democrats supported the war and only condemned Morton, then "they suddenly failed to attend their local party meetings in the spring of 1863."[60] Ultimately, Sylvester said, "Historians must still base their conclusions on partisan newspaper accounts, political propaganda, and speeches and correspondence written during turbulent times."[61]

Current scholarship has undermined Klement's claims that secret societies were the figment of the imaginations of Northern politicians and Union army officers, and have called into question the historian's research methods and findings. A 2015 study by historian Stephen E. Towne examined the intensive U.S. Army intelligence operations in the Midwest during the war and its efforts to uncover subversive organizations and activities. Towne noted that based on the reliable evidence uncovered by investigators, "upheaval and violence were close to the surface throughout the region as ideologically driven secret political groups threatened large-scale unrest."[62]

Whether the KGC, the OAK, and the SOL were extensive underground organizations, or simply the reflection of intense resentment on the part of southern Indiana citizens toward the imposition of Republican political goals, the result was the same. Southern Indiana was a cauldron of boiling emotion that often spilled over into violence. Families were split, towns divided, and reputations smeared.

While Morton was able to keep the Copperheads off balance with the specter of the secret societies, he was not initially able to turn his strategy into electoral success for his new Union Party. The Democrats swept the fall 1862 elections, taking seven of nine statewide races and seven of eleven congressional seats, along with both houses of the legislature. Scott County voters continued their recent habit of sending Democrats to the general assembly and to Congress. Copperhead politicians such as Cravens, the Kimberlins' congressman (the second district included Clark, Crawford, Floyd, Harrison, Orange, Perry, Scott, and Washington Counties) took full advantage. Cravens beat the Republican James G. May 10,911 to 6,211. In Scott County, Cravens won 800 to 562 votes.[63] The Union Party was now seriously wounded.

The Democratic sweep in the fall 1862 elections spelled more trouble for Morton. The Democrats used their new power in the legislature to embarrass the governor and to chide Lincoln for a failed strategy. Peace Democrats introduced several resolutions, professing that peace could never be accomplished by the sword. Others urged compromise and a unilateral armistice. The final report from the Senate Committee on Federal Relations bitterly criticized Lincoln and Emancipation, but also condemned secession.[64]

The 1863 legislative session ended with a Republican walkout over the Democrats' attempt to divide authority for the militia between the governor and other state elected officials. Morton called it an act of treason.[65] But the low point for Morton and the Republican Party came a few months later on July 1, coincidentally the opening day of the Battle of Gettysburg. The Democratic State Auditor, Joseph Ristine, refused to pay bills because the session ended without the passage of the appropriation legislation. When Morton appealed to the Indiana Supreme Court for help, the court rebuffed him. What followed was a constitutional and political standoff that almost resulted in violence. Morton, with his personal guarantee, immediately borrowed money from New York banks, appealed to Secretary of War Edwin Stanton to take up some of the state's military expenses, and asked friends such as Calvin Fletcher and Republican county officials to make personal contributions. In the meantime, General John

Coburn was in Indianapolis with a regiment of troops. Coburn offered to break into the state treasury to confiscate the necessary funds. Morton declined Coburn's offer and maintained the borrowing strategy for two years, keeping the state's cash in a safe in his office.[66] Morton's bold move led Democrats to compare him to Charles I of England who defied Parliament and personally financed the government of England for eleven years, from 1629 to 1640. Charles later paid for his audacity with his head.[67]

Morton kept his head, and his extraconstitutional tactics kept the war economy running, but he was not able to win over the hearts of Hoosiers living south of the National Road. Copperhead rejection of the shifting justification for the war sparked an intense backlash, which evolved into violence across southern Indiana. The *Madison Daily and Evening Courier* reported on February 24, 1863, that a "grand pow-wow was held at the courthouse in Lexington . . . the old brick walls rang for an hour with the stentorian voice of Hon. William H. English. He said the war was an abolitionist war waged expressly for the extermination of slavery, and it must be stopped."[68]

The young diarist of Lexington, Sarah Waldschmidt Young Bovard, continued to observe events in her little world. She got her war news from the *Cincinnati Gazette*. Local reaction occurred daily: "The Butternuts are getting very saucy in Indiana," she wrote,[69] just two weeks after Congress passed a federal draft bill. One month later Bovard recounted, "The Butternuts had a meeting last night at the Franklin school house and Isaac Mayfield had a Union one at the McClain school."[70] A week later, "two Union men were killed in a riot and rebel mobs in Brown County."[71] In October she noted, "The Copperheads meet in the woods up at Cat Wallow. M. Eyfelds tried to kill an abolitionist."[72] On Thanksgiving Day 1863, the ultimate sign of a split in Bovard's family over the war: "Mother roasted a turkey for Margaret. Don't want anybody but secesh to help eat it."[73]

James Adams of Brookville served as a colonel in the Forty-Fifth Indiana. He wrote often to his sister, Catherine Allison, who had a Copperhead husband, J. D. Each time Catherine received a letter from James, her husband became enraged and confiscated the letter. On May 17, 1864, James wrote to Catherine: "I have thought considerable about your situation . . . I will give you a plan. I will place that which is strictly private on one sheet, and what he may see on another. You can secret the one and hand him the other."[74] Before the war was over, Catherine had divorced J. D.

In the summer of 1863, when the federal draft began, correspondence between Doctor John McPheeters, assistant surgeon in the Twenty-Third Indiana (one of the Kimberlin regiments) and his wife, Mollie, turned to the draft. Mollie wrote on June 15: "some of the copperheads talk more boldly. A great many in Stamper's Creek Township say they will shoot the man who comes to enroll their names. Port Cornwell was appointed enroller, but declined the appointment."[75] Two weeks later, George McPheeters, John's brother, wrote: "There seems to be a determination in a number of localities to resist the conscript. Extensive organizations for that purpose. A few enrolling officers have been shot. The enrollment has been stopped by armed force in a great many places."[76]

In an undated letter to Governor Morton, Doctor James Hosea of Scott County described a Copperhead meeting at the Austin schoolhouse, eight miles northwest of Lexington in Scott County, where fifty-four men gathered. The chairman was a Mr. Sirrup. According to Hosea, the men pledged not to help out any families whose sons have gone to fight, and to protect deserters.[77]

The hysterical suspicion was mutual. Kenneth Stampp wrote that "loyal citizens lived in panicky fear of their own neighbors, and lumped all dissidents into the single category of traitors."[78] Violence and intimidation suppressed logical debate. Reminiscing seventy years after the war, Julie LeClerc of Vevay noted that "the little town of Veevay [sic] was divided between Unionists and southern sympathizers. When Jason Brown, state representative from Dearborn County, came to speak in support of Vallandigham, the Ohio Peace Democrat, the Unionists element rushed into the LeClerc house, and threatened to swing him from the nearest lamp post."[79]

A similar story involved the annual July 4 celebration on the Lexington town square. Interviewed in the *Scott County Journal* in 1924, Alice Jones recalled "the 1863 celebration was disrupted by Copperheads shouting hooray for Jefferson Davis. One was attacked by an elderly lady with a parasol."[80] That was the day after Gettysburg and Vicksburg fell, and it was three days before Confederate General John Hunt Morgan crossed into Indiana.

Morgan's Raid

When Morgan crossed the Ohio River at Brandenburg on July 7, 1863, with 2,400 mounted soldiers, southern Indiana was unprepared. The Scott County Home Guard had been sent to protect the federal depot at Jeffersonville. Morgan made short work of the feeble defenses at Corydon, killing several home guards, stealing horses, and trashing local businesses. He turned east at Salem, reunified his forces at Vienna in Scott County, and approached Lexington on July 10. Ira Mace of

Confederate general John Hunt Morgan. He was killed on September 4, 1864, after being shot in the back by Union cavalrymen while attempting to escape during a raid on Greeneville, Tennessee.

Lexington recalled in 1937 that old men and boys set up an 1812 cannon near the cemetery but fled without firing. "Copperheads, Butternuts, and Knights of the Golden Circle were in a majority in these parts of southern Indiana," said Mace. "I saw my father pass through our yard with a rifle in each hand. The extra gun belonged to a neighbor who sympathized with the Confederates. He refused to join the bushwhackers so they compelled him to surrender his gun."[81] Two thousand Union troops occupied Lexington the next day as Morgan headed for Ohio.

There is no credible evidence that Morgan communicated with Hoosiers in planning the raid, or that he hoped to get help from sympathetic locals. If he had, he would have been disappointed. Residents of Harrison, Washington, and Scott Counties reacted more with anger than with sympathy at having their horses stolen and protection money demanded. There are only a few anecdotal indicators of any cooperation. Samuel Demaree reportedly joined the Confederate army in Kentucky well before the raid and rode with Morgan through Indiana. He was captured in Ohio,

IHS, P 455

General John Hunt Morgan's Confederate raiders burn and pillage the depot and stores at Salem, Indiana, on July 10, 1863, in this Frank Leslie's Illustrated Newspaper *drawing.*

paroled, and lived thereafter with his family in Johnson County.[82] Harrison Gookins of the Thirty-seventh Indiana, a native of Delaware in Ripley County, wrote from Descherd, Tennessee, on July 28, 1863: "I heard old Bill Hartley, Ed Ferrer and some more had gone off with Morgan. I would like to see them and help hang them."[83]

Unified on Color

Added to active disobedience toward the draft was an almost universal rejection of the recruitment of African American troops into the Union army early in 1863. The *Madison Courier, New Albany Ledger,* and smaller papers throughout the second congressional district criticized the arming of African Americans because they feared the instant leverage they would have with their white counterparts when they returned home. Editors thought African American veterans would be given special treatment for their service when looking for jobs. By the end of 1863, however, sentiment on the black soldier issue had mellowed. Hoosiers realized that for every African American soldier at the front, that meant one less white man had to go and fight.[84]

The shifting feelings on black troops were typical of the moral dilemma Hoosiers of both political parties faced. While few Hoosiers believed that African Americans should be held in bondage, at the same time they believed that blacks should be segregated in political, social, and military affairs. They wanted African Americans to be free. They just did not want to mix with them. Hoosier sentiment may best have been summed up by Lincoln himself when he said, "Just because I did not want a Negro woman for a slave, I do not necessarily want her for my wife."[85]

Prelude to Battle

While southern Indiana boiled, brothers Jacob T. and John J., and cousins, William H. H. and Benjamin, sat before Colliersville, Tennessee, on January 10, 1863, waiting for the expected spring offensive.[86] Isaac Newton Kimberlin (Jacob's older brother) was nearby with the Seventh Missouri Volunteers. It is not known how or why Isaac enrolled in a Missouri unit, except for his matter of fact statement in an affidavit addressed to the Commissioner of Pensions, and signed by Isaac on March 11, 1891. Isaac simply stated: "I enlisted in Co. "G", 7 Reg., M.O. Inf., May 20, 1861, discharged March 1, 1866."[87] His statement is corroborated by the official record of the Civil War when documenting his later heroism.[88] He may have signed up while in Saint Louis on business. We also know that the Seventh Missouri fought alongside the Twenty-third Indiana at Shiloh, and was consolidated with the Eleventh Missouri in December 1864.

Writing along a railroad track between LaGrange and Memphis, William reported to Jacob "R" back home: "It is supposed that we will go to Vicksburg before long wher thare is a hevy fight expected and it is likely that we will be thare to see the fun. . . . I will send you some peas that grow in this country they are called Whipowill peas they should be planted about the 15th of April . . . they are very nice."[89] William's brother, Benjamin, wrote to Jacob "R" two weeks later from Memphis: "I have not much hope of seeing any of you unless I should live to serve my time out in this war"[90]

On February 21, 1863, the Twenty-third Indiana boarded boats to go down river toward Vicksburg, landing at Lake Providence, Louisiana.[91] News of the draft reached camp quickly. On March 14 William told Jacob "R" in a letter: "I want you to tell brother John and Hopper if they see that they cant get rid of the draft I want them to volunteer and come to this regiment . . . that way they can draw their bounty money."[92]

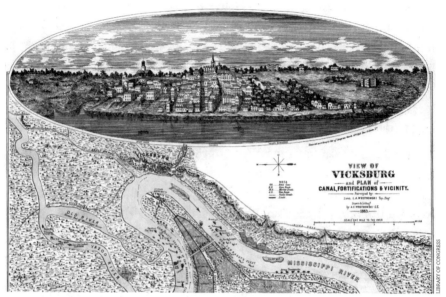

An 1863 view of Vicksburg, Mississippi, showing the city and its fortifications and the deployment of the Union fleet along the Mississippi River.

Domestic affairs crept into the Kimberlin correspondence as the Twenty-third awaited its marching orders. On April 1 Benjamin tried to settle a family dispute in a letter to his sister, Elizabeth. It seemed that his father-in-law, Luther Starkes, was charging Benjamin to board his own daughter, Benjamin's wife, Sarah, while Benjamin was at war. "I have always paid my just debts so far and I hope to be able to pay them hereafter," wrote Benjamin. "I expect it will be a snipes bill of the longest kind . . . he is so prejudiced against me that he could not do me justice. . . I will make it long in another way."[93]

In one of his longest letters of the war, John "J" wrote on April 12 of constant boredom and reflected on everything from "Negroes" to traitors:

> Gen. Thomas is here for the purpose of raising a Negro regt. and giving commissions to officers to command them. They are to be stationed on these vacated farms . . . to raise subsistence for the army and to keep down the guerrilors along the river. . . . I think it is the thing the Government can do with them for we do not want them in the North I am certain and there is hundreds and thousands of acres that aint doing any body any good unless it is tilled by the negros. . . . I will fight the rebs with Negroes wolves panthers or elephants, and if I had 10,000 elephants I would turn them all loose

and let them thrash the devel out of them. . . . I know we are accused being abolishionist thieves and murderers in our own state, I care not what burlesks may be heaped upon us we are for the union as it is and constitution as it was [a transposition of a political slogan] . . . we will show our old copperheads at home that our old flag shall not be insulted.[94]

John "J" got his wish. On April 22 volunteers were sought from several regiments to board gunboats to run the Warrenton and Vicksburg batteries. John's brother, Isaac, with the Seventh Missouri, was among the volunteers. John Hardin of Company E, Twenty-third Indiana, described the run in a letter home: "six of our transports run the blockade the night of the 22nd. We lost one boat, it was sunk. The rest went through without much damage. The officers that belong to the boats would not run the blockade so they had to make details . . . our boys were anxious to go . . . only 10 cannonballs and about 2,000 rifle balls went through the boat."[95] Isaac was singled out in the after-action report of Colonel W. S. Oliver, commander of the steamer *Tigress*, the lead boat, for staying at his post as "a very heavy shot in the stern knocked away three knees and two planks, making an opening of at least 4 feet in her hull . . . our men put cotton bags into such holes as might be made by their shot. The *Tigress* received

A print depicting the Siege of Vicksburg, showing Union tents and underground bunkers in the foreground. In the distance are Union rifle pits and along the ridge are Confederate forts and earthworks.

in all thirty-five shots, fourteen of which struck her hull, the last one causing her to fill and settle fast."[96] Isaac survived, but tragedy loomed ahead for the Kimberlins.

Vicksburg Campaign

Isaac's heroics were critical to the eventual success of General Ulysses S. Grant's strategy to capture Vicksburg. The city, long believed to be even more important than Memphis and New Orleans in controlling the Mississippi River, had withstood three attempts by Union armies to force its capitulation. Both sides agreed on Vicksburg's strategic role. Confederate president Jefferson Davis described Vicksburg as "the nailhead that held the two halves of the Confederacy together."[97] Lincoln told a gathering of general officers, "Vicksburg is the key. The war can never be brought to a close until that key is in our pocket."[98]

Grant was under great pressure to produce results at Vicksburg. As spring 1863 blossomed in the bayous, Grant decided to move south along

Marker at the Vicksburg National Military Park honoring the Indiana Twenty-third Infantry Regiment

Artist Theodore R. Davis made these sketches showing views of the different stages of the Battle of Raymond fought on May 12, 1863.

the Arkansas shore opposite Vicksburg to a point across from Grand Gulf, Mississippi, where he hoped to land 22,000 infantrymen, including the Twenty-third Indiana. Rear Admiral David Dixon Porter's gunboats failed to silence the defenses at Grand Gulf, so Grant marched his army five miles south and completed one of the largest amphibious landings in American military history at Bruinsburg, Mississippi, from April 30 to May 1, 1863.[99] Grant was now in position to encircle Vicksburg from the east and to lay siege indefinitely. But first, Union forces had to fight their way off the beachhead.

Bruinsburg to Vicksburg

Confederate scouts quickly alerted Generals John Bowen and Edward Baldwin, who rushed forces from Port Gibson and Grand Gulf to the Bayou Pierre, a nearly impenetrable entanglement of undergrowth divided by deep ravines and located west of Port Gibson. On May 1, in a battle known by two names, Port Gibson and Thompson's Hill, the Twenty-third helped turn the right flank of Bowen's Confederate line, forcing the Rebels to fall back through the bayou and Port Gibson. John Hardin was

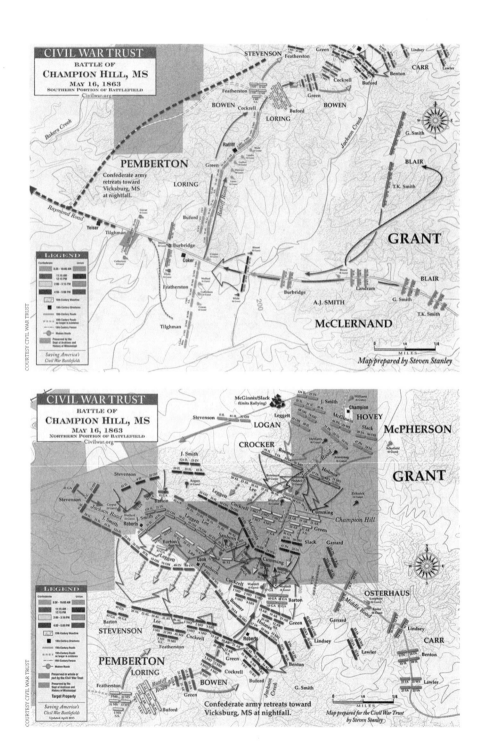

CIVIL WAR TRUST
BATTLE OF
CHAMPION HILL, MS
MAY 16, 1863
SOUTHERN PORTION OF BATTLEFIELD
Civilwar.org

LEGEND

PEMBERTON
Confederate army
retreats toward
Vicksburg, MS
at nightfall.

GRANT

McCLERNAND

BLAIR

*Saving America's
Civil War Battlefields*

Map prepared by Steven Stanley

CIVIL WAR TRUST
BATTLE OF
CHAMPION HILL, MS
MAY 16, 1863
NORTHERN PORTION OF BATTLEFIELD
Civilwar.org

McPHERSON

HOVEY

GRANT

LOGAN

CROCKER

OSTERHAUS

CARR

LEGEND

STEVENSON

PEMBERTON
LORING

BOWEN

Confederate army retreats toward
Vicksburg, MS at nightfall.

*Saving America's
Civil War Battlefields*
Updated April 2015

*Map prepared for the Civil War Trust
by Steven Stanley*

A print showing Union soldiers in trench and behind wooden walls and gabions as an assault is made on Fort Hill during the siege of Vicksburg.

captured there, and William H. was cut down by troops of the Twentieth Alabama under Colonel Isham Garrott.[100] William H. H. was one of ten members of the Twenty-third Indiana killed that day.[101]

Grant's next tactical objective was the railroad connecting the capital of Jackson, Mississippi, to Vicksburg. He moved his army slowly northeast, scouting for the cavalry of Nathan Bedford Forrest and the army of Earl Van Dorn, a native of Port Gibson, as he went. For the second time in six months, Grant split his army at Rocky Springs, sending most of his troops toward Jackson while General John Logan's division, including the Twenty-third, moved directly north toward the railroad.[102] On May 12, 1863, as Logan's forces topped a ridge south of Raymond, Mississippi, they saw Confederate forces under General John Gregg blocking their intended crossing of Fourteen Mile Creek. The land between the ridge and the creek is an open plain sloping toward thick woods camouflaging the creek. The Twenty-Third advanced east of the road, next to the 124th Illinois, but became detached and "alone met the onslaught of five confederate regiments, two on one side and three on another, being almost entirely surrounded . . . with fixed bayonets and clubbed muskets, they successfully emerged from what seemed to be an almost hopeless position, fell back to the main line, reformed, and continued in the engagement."[103] Benjamin was shot dead by soldiers of the Third Tennessee before he could reach the creek, about midday.[104] Regimental physician McPheeters described the battle to his wife, Mollie: "Been in four hard fights, one at Thompson's Hill about which I wrote you, and the fight at Raymond, in which our regt. fought and lost guite a number killed and wounded."[105] Benjamin never got to pay his wife's rent.

Writing of his cousin's death, Jacob T. Kimberlin told Jacob "R":

> I was in the hospital at Grand Gulf when the battle of Raymond was fought . . . it was there that your brother Benjamin was killed. . . . William having ben killed at Thompson's Hill. . . . Raymond was a desperate encounter. Far hotter than our regiment was ever in before or since. The Rebels were quickly driven back but not until they had killed 16, wounded more than one hundred, and captured 23. And all of this was done in the astonishly short space of a few minutes . . . all of Ben's things were lost. Everything being taken from his pocket by the Rebels. He was buried by the side of Lt. Henry C. Dietz who was killed about the same time and but a short distance from the same place. The graves of both men are marked with their names and the regt. to which they belonged.[106]

When Grant arrived at Jackson, he found most of the Confederate troops had evacuated the city and moved west to guard the approaches to the Black River. Grant's troops torched Jackson and reunited with Logan's division on May 16, 1863, near Bolton, along the Southern Railroad of Mississippi. There, near the crest of Champion's Hill, the forces of Van Dorn fought desperately to block Logan's and General Alvin Hovey's divisions from reaching the Black River. During a five-hour battle, Union troops took and retook the fields around the Champion House, with the Twenty-third Indiana, under Colonel William Sanderson (of General John E. Smith's brigade), eventually pushing General Seth Barton's Fortieth Georgia into a general retreat. As at Raymond four days earlier, Confederate forces were not defeated decisively but withdrew from the field toward Vicksburg.[107] After one more battle of moderate severity at the Black River crossing on May 17, 1863, Van Dorn's forces holed up inside the defensive perimeter at Vicksburg and awaited a long siege.

Vicksburg

The Vicksburg defenses consisted of massive batteries on the bluffs overlooking the Mississippi River, and a crescent on the north, east, and south perimeters, consisting of nine forts connected by a system of trenches. The Twenty-third Indiana was in the front line of the siege at Vicksburg, stationed along the White House Road, directly within range of Confederate troops manning the Third Louisiana Redan. On May 22, 1863, three days after a hastily ordered assault on the Vicksburg works had failed, Grant ordered a general assault along a three-mile front. The Twenty-third, in tandem with the Forty-fifth Illinois, gained the crest of the Third Louisiana Redan, only to be pushed back to the base. On June 25, in an eerie precursor to the infamous mine explosion at Petersburg one year later, Logan's division finished an excavation under the same redan, and ignited 2,200 pounds of black powder. Again, the Twenty-Third rushed into the crater and fought for the breech with bayonets and hand grenades. Logan sent regiment after regiment into the crater for more than twenty-six hours, but the assault failed and both sides settled down into trench warfare again.[108]

Union general William Tecumseh Sherman and his staff pose for the camera at federal Fort Number 7 near Atlanta, Georgia, July 18, 1864.

Starved and diseased more than they were defeated, Confederate troops under General John Pemberton surrendered on July 4, 1863, one day after Robert E. Lee's Confederate army lost at Gettysburg. From May 21 to July 4, 1863, the Twenty-third lost fifty-five men killed and wounded.[109] Jacob T. was one of those wounded. Writing from an unnamed regimental hospital on June 13, he told Jacob R: "I am at present in our regimental hospital from the effects of a wound I received on the 4th instant. I rejoined the regiment after having left the hospital [Grand Gulf] on the 3rd June, and on the ensuing day was shot through both hips while going for water. I have been in the hospital ever since. I am doing quite well, and hope to be able to inform you of my rapid recovery soon."[110] Jacob T.'s luck did not hold. On August 2, his older brother, Isaac, wrote home to cousins Jacob F. and Jacob "R": "I have bad news to write this evening. Brother Jacob died at 9 o'clock this morning and will be intered some time tomorrow at Greenville. Sister Mary will be at viena on next Wednesday and warrent I will try to meet her there. . . . I expect to come with her if I can get off . . . excuse these few lines, and consider me your cousin, I.N. Kimberlin"[111]

Momentum and the March

Morton's and the Republican Party's fortunes changed for the better after the Union victories at Gettysburg and Vicksburg. There was a sense in Indiana that the war was finally turning in favor of the Union. While resistance to the draft persisted, and Morton continued to suppress opposition newspapers under the cover of General Order Number 38 (editors in Plymouth and South Bend, for example, were arrested because of their editorials), the Indiana economy continued to chug along and the flow of volunteers made the draft almost unnecessary.[112] Most of the surviving members of the Twenty-third Indiana, for example, reenlisted for "three years more, or until the close of the war."[113]

The Twenty-Third stayed at or near Vicksburg through the winter of 1863, joining other regiments from time to time for sorties to Monroe, Louisiana; Canton, Missouri; and Meridian, Mississippi, to destroy railroads and to disrupt the ability of Confederate troops to concentrate for a spring campaign. The threat of a land-based Confederate attack was pervasive. Isaac participated in reinforcement of the fortifications around Vicksburg after he returned to his regiment from an illness, writing on November 3, 1863, his birthday, "We will Soon have the Breast works

A print showing the contenders for the 1864 presidential election, including the Republican ticket of Abraham Lincoln and Andrew Johnson, and the Democratic ticket of George B. McClellan and George H. Pendleton. Bust portraits of the previous presidents run around the edge of the print.

General James McPherson's death at the Battle of Atlanta made him the second highest ranking Union officer killed during the war.

done, the most formidable in the united states all the Southern Army could not Shake it or take the place once complete."[114]

Just after Christmas, Isaac wrote home to an engaged Jacob R., in anticipation of a leave: "Though I am very satisfied where I am yet I believe I could enjoy a visit to old Scott for a few Days. Jake I heard that you was about to put the thing through with Sally and I believe it is pretty well founded. Now Jake I have one word to say on this subject, and that is, Don't try on your vest until I come home Jake I weigh 165 I am as fat as a bear and still thriving As I expect to see you Soon I will come by."[115] In March 1864 the regiment left Vicksburg for New Albany by boat for its official thirty-day "veterans leave."

We do not know how the Kimberlins and their cousins, the Whit-lachs and Houghs, spent their leave in Scott County. Because they were at home there was no need to write letters. It is safe to assume that they did exactly what they had looked forward to doing: catch up with the women, help out on the farm, and give the family more details about how their sons and brothers had died. While at home, the war continued without them. Forrest captured the old headquarters of the Twenty-third, Pa-ducah, in late March 1864. On April 12 Forrest captured Fort Pillow and massacred several hundred "colored" troops after they had surrendered. Farther south that same day, the Twenty-third's fighting comrades, the XVII Corps, helped disperse Confederate General Tom Green's cavalry division as it tried to capture Union transports and armament on the banks of the Red River at Pleasant Hill Landing.

Amidst the various military campaigns, campaigns of another sort were also being played out: the re-election campaigns of Lincoln and Morton. Despite the attempt of Peace Democrats such as Daniel Voorhees to promote the candidacy of General George B. McClellan for president in 1864,[116] Indiana historian Emma Lou Thornbrough noted that "war weary Indianians generally accepted the re-nomination of Lincoln without great enthusiasm."[117] That did not mean Morton was at ease. He stepped up his warnings about traitorous activities, culminating in the arrest of Lambdin Milligan and his alleged fellow plotters of the Northwest Con-spiracy. Morton justified his actions on the basis of accomplishing a higher moral goal. "If we use all the means within our reach, it is within the power of the Union Party to save the state," he wrote.[118] The timing was perfect for Morton, considering that the October election (November for

General Sherman's troops destroy Confederate railroad tracks and buildings on its March to the Sea through Georgia from November 15 to December 21, 1864.

president) came just weeks after General William T. Sherman's victory at Atlanta and General Philip Sheridan's victory in the Shenandoah Valley. These triumphs for the Union, combined with the uproar about the "treason trials" by a military court in Indianapolis, made it very difficult for anyone to boldly announce against Morton without looking like a fool at best or a traitor at worst.

Morton also strategized to maximize the assured friendly vote of Hoosier soldiers in the field. In letters to Lincoln and Secretary of War Stanton, Morton urged mass furloughs for Indiana troops, arguing that without their vote his future and Lincoln's as well were precarious. Stanton opposed the furloughs, but Morton prevailed on Lincoln to allow sick and wounded soldiers a thirty-day reprieve. The governor sent agents to visit Indiana regiments to poll them on the presidential and gubernatorial races, and to encourage those eligible to come home. One aide suggested to Morton not to bring home the Fifty-ninth regiment because its members and most of its officers were "coppers."[119]

Posted with the Seventh Missouri at the mouth of the White River in Arkansas, Isaac opined on the election in a September 25, 1864, letter to cousin Jacob R.: "Well Jake perhaps you would like to know my opinion about Abe and the election. Well If I had a hundred thousand Dollars I would bet that Abe would be re-elected. And if I had that many votes I would Shove them all to Abrahams bosom, the officers took a vote of our Division and little Mc got about one vote out of every hundred, friemont [Charles Fremont] none."[120]

In the end, 9,000 Hoosier soldiers returned home to vote. Morton probably did not need the furlough program to seal his victory. Indiana went for him by a margin of 20,000 votes. Republicans won eight of eleven congressional seats, almost a complete reversal of 1862, even defeating Morton's nemesis, Voorhees, in his re-election bid for Congress.[121] Republicans also retook both houses of the Indiana legislature. Calvin Fletcher said anyone who voted for McClellan and the Democrats was a "traitor and a copperhead."[122]

Judging by the Scott County vote in 1864, there were plenty of traitors and copperheads in residence there. The county maintained its political tradition after 1850 of electing to local, state, and federal office Democrats who were fiercely independent of mainstream thinking, while generally maintaining a loyal if not effusively pro-Union attitude as secession and civil war occurred. Men such as Cravens, Bright, English, and Heffren kept up their loyalist behavior while excoriating Lincoln, Morton, Stanton, and other Republican leaders as men willing to go beyond the Constitution to preserve a Union that should not be preserved without the consent of their southern brethren.

While Scott County landed solidly in the Democrat camp, the underlying split between those who believed in "the Constitution as it is, the Union as it was," and those who believed that their true interests lay with the South, was never resolved during the Civil War. Scott County's sentiment can best be described as a strange comingling of philosophies that might seem contradictory to an outsider. A Scott County motto of 1864 might have read, "Union, yes, but Southern at heart and in soul."

An Awful Price for Union

The two primary Kimberlin regiments, the Twenty-third Indiana and Sixty-sixth Indiana, eventually rejoined on June, 9, 1864, at Ackworth, Georgia, to fight under Sherman in his Georgia campaign and his March to the Sea. Both regiments saw action at Kennesaw Mountain, Nickajack Creek, Peach Tree Creek, and the battle of Atlanta, where General James McPherson was killed.[123] Six more Kimberlins would be strewn on battlefields and in hospitals across the South. Those who lived marched with Robert Armstrong of Horner's Chapel, Indiana, and Doctor McPheeters of Livonia through North Carolina and Richmond and on to Washington, D.C. In his war diary, Armstrong wrote about arriving on battlefields (Altoona) and "being almost sickened at the sight."[124] But there were lighter moments as well. McPheeters wrote to Mollie of the celebration of Lee's surrender, in camp at Goldsboro, North Carolina, on April 9, 1865: "some 15 or 20 boys from the 22nd Indiana came here last night dressed in women's clothes. . . . Brought their music along for a dance . . . their spitting tobacco juice was no evidence that they were not women . . . they danced till they got tired, then went home highly pleased."[125] One of Armstong's last diary entries simply reads: "spent the day at the Capitol and the Patent Office, get some pictures for my album."[126]

5

Home and Away

The Scott County that the Kimberlins and their cousins returned to in June 1865 was not significantly different than when they left. During the four years of war, families struggled to maintain the agricultural economy with fewer farmhands to plow the fields and bring in the harvest. Because Scott County was not home to large manufacturing facilities critical to the war effort, the wealth that some Hoosiers amassed never trickled down to county residents.

One Kimberlin, Jacob "R.," to whom most of the family's surviving Civil War letters were sent, was able to provide some family leadership on the farm because of his staggered service in the war. He was given advice from his brothers in the field when he was home, and he in turn gave advice when he was on the battlefield: "I will inclose Some muskuline grape Seed in this letter which you can plant this fall, they grow about as large as a fox grape. And are a very nice fruit, they are ripe now and the woods here is livid with them I wish I could send you Some of the grapes and then I know you would not neglect them."[1]

In many ways, however, everything had changed for the Kimberlins. They had lost ten brothers and cousins during the war. Like returning soldiers from all wars, they had to rebuild marriages and careers. For some, the end of the war was an opportunity to pull up roots and explore the land to the west that many of their new friends from the war had told them about.

How did the Kimberlins fare in the decades after the Civil War? Did the stability brought by peace provide a launching point for family prosperity and good fortune? Census records provide very limited information about the fate of the Kimberlins. Thanks to pension records in the U.S.

Lexington served as the first county seat of Scott County. In 1821 a two-story brick court-house was constructed at a cost of $4,500. When the county seat moved to Scottsburg in 1874, the courthouse became a school that lasted until 1889.

National Archives, however, we are able to reconstruct the postwar lives of many of the family members. As one might suspect, the stories that the archives reveal provide fascinating witness to the triumphs and travails of the Kimberlins and their descendants as late as the 1960s.

Congress passed several pension bills during and after the Civil War that provided for small monthly pensions for disabled soldiers, their widows, and surviving children. The monthly stipend depended on the degree of disability and length of service. For a disabled veteran or a widow with children, eight to twelve dollars per month could mean the difference between economic survival and dependency on the generosity of relatives or neighbors. Some, such as Clarissa Meeks Kimberlin, the wife of David Kimberlin, filed for a widow's pension within a few months of her husband's death at the battle of Richmond, Kentucky, in August 1862.[2] Most, however, applied for disability pensions well after the war, sometimes as late as thirty years after returning home.

Delayed applications created significant obstacles to obtaining a pension. Affidavits from fellow soldiers, physicians, family members, and neighbors as to the cause of the disability and the degree to which it affected the applicant's ability to earn a living, were reviewed by a local review board and adjudicated by pension officials in Washington, D.C. Joseph Hough (a Kimberlin cousin), for example, did not file for a pension until 1884, and then claimed that sunstroke suffered while he marched with the 145th Indiana Regiment from Resaca, Georgia, to Cartersville, Georgia, left him unable to earn a living. Hough submitted affidavits from his first lieutenant in Company E and others in the company vaguely recalling Hough being taken from the roadside by ambulance. Family members testified that he suffered continually from headaches and fevers. Hough's petition was approved at a reduced level.[3]

While a delayed pension application caused stress and sometimes hardship for the applicant and his family, it produced a treasure trove of documentation on the soldier's postwar life that today serves as a significant source of information for the historian or genealogical researcher. Very detailed medical exams, marriage and work records, property holdings, and family relationships are all preserved, most often in handwritten form. They collectively help complete the puzzle from which we learn how these veterans lived and died after the war.

Survival of the Mundane

The Kimberlins and their cousins quickly blended back into Scott County society after the war. While the community was still dealing with the emotion of the Union victory and the assassination of President Abraham Lincoln, the Kimberlin veterans resumed their prewar pursuits as farmers and coopers, and in one case, a preacher. Some Kimberlins began to spread out to neighboring counties of Washington and Jennings, and as far north as Indianapolis. A few headed for Illinois and the upper Midwest. All maintained family connections to Scott County, and some returned from time to time to live or to visit. For most of the Kimberlins, postwar life was a mundane routine of economic survival that is not much different from the stories of millions of veterans to this day. Marriages were pledged, children were born, jobs were gained and lost, and personal health was always at the forefront of discussion. The stories of five Kimberlins are worthy of further study, either because of how they lived their postwar lives or because the volume of information available provides the means to track them with significant detail. Each deserves his own attention. The remainder of the extended Kimberlin family is dealt with briefly in the appendices.

A War Hero's Odyssey

Isaac Newton Kimberlin, son of Jacob J. Kimberlin and Elizabeth Old-ham (appendix A), enlisted in Company G of the Seventh Missouri Infantry on May 20, 1861, at Saint Louis, more than a month before any other Kimberlin entered service.[4] Isaac's Missouri regiment served nearby the Twenty-third Indiana as part of General George McPherson's XVII Corps throughout his term, including the Battle of Shiloh and the Vicksburg campaign from Port Gibson to the fall of Vicksburg. Along the way he communicated regularly with his cousin, Jacob "R," and informed the family of the deaths of his brothers in the Twenty-third Indiana, Jacob "T" and John "J," and of his cousins, Benjamin F. Kimberlin and William H. H. Kimberlin.

The five-foot, eight inch Isaac weighed 165 pounds and had hazel eyes and light hair. He was recognized in official reports for his bravery in running the batteries at Vicksburg aboard the transport *Tigress*, and in an affidavit by his company commander, Captain A. I. Judy. "This was an excellent soldier who volunteered to run the blockade at Vicksburg when the supply transports were run past."[5] The Seventh Missouri was consolidated with the Eleventh Missouri in December 1864, after which Isaac participated in chasing John Bell Hood to the Tennessee River after the Battle of Nashville and in the capture of Mobile on April 12, 1865, two days before Lincoln was assassinated.[6]

MICHAEL S. MURPHY

John Napoleon Kimberlin

After Isaac was mustered out of the army on March 1, 1866, he settled in Marysville, Indiana, for a short time before moving to Salem, Indiana, where he began an itinerant life as a gardener, working small plots for people who could afford the luxury of that type of help. Following one year in Salem, Isaac moved, for six months, to Greenville, Indiana, then upon the invitation of friends traveled to Helena, Montana, for two years. In 1871 Isaac moved to Saint Louis, where he stayed three years. He was off to

Chicago for two years in 1874, then to Lockport, Illinois, for one year and on to Minneapolis in 1877.[7] In Minneapolis Isaac continued his career as a gardener and met Julia Crowe, wife of John Crowe. We do not know much about Julia, but we do know that she divorced her husband and married Isaac in the same month, September 1888. A daughter, Jessie May, was born to Isaac and Julia on December 30, 1889.

Less than a year later, apparently suffering the effects of wartime disabilities, Isaac moved with his family back to Mitchell, Indiana, in Lawrence County. It was from there, while living with his brother, Doctor H. L. Kimberlin, that he first filed for a Civil War "invalid" pension, claiming "deafness and disease of lungs."[8] In early 1891 H. L. diagnosed Isaac with "pulmonary consumption." Affidavits filed on his behalf, including one from fellow soldier, Clinton Shaw, confirmed that on May 22, 1863, while Isaac was supporting a battery at Vicksburg, a shell exploded near him and caused him to go deaf for several weeks. Isaac's petition for a pension was granted.

Two years later, Isaac was living in Olney, Illinois, with custody of Jessie. His wife Julia's whereabouts at that time are unknown. We do know that Isaac filed for and was granted a divorce from Julia, a native of Germany, on November 22, 1893. The Richland County Court decreed that "Julia Kimberlin has been guilty of willful desertion for the space of two years and over and been guilty of living in an open state of adultery with one Otto Keefer . . . and that she is a woman of low and vulgar habits, and no fit person to have the care custody and education of their said child Jessie May Kimberlin."[9] Isaac was granted custody of Jessie, but his relief was short-lived. He died in Olney, Illinois, just three months later, on February 6, 1894.

Jessie's problem was just beginning. Upon her father's death custody of the four-year-old girl was transferred to her cousin, James H. Kimberlin, himself a Civil War veteran, in Richland County, Illinois. The next thirteen years are lost to history but Jessie was again the subject of government proceedings when she applied for continuation of her "helpless minor" pension in January 1907. By this time Jessie was seventeen years old, five feet two, and 102 pounds, with light brown hair and hazel eyes, just like her dad. Her pension had expired. Jessie's family and friends came to her rescue. Her aunt, Mary Kimberlin Abbott, who had cared for Jessie as a little girl, filed an affidavit claiming that Jessie

FIND A GRAVE

Jessie May Kimberlin

was "never able to attend a full term of school."[10] Affidavits were also filed on her behalf by Mary Stucker, Nancy Hardy, and her cousin, James H. Kimberlin. On her own behalf, Jessie testified: "During the winter of 1904 and 1905, I took a pain in my right lung, whenever I would draw my breath it was like sticking a sharp instrument into it. I will never forget the day I quit school in February . . . I couldn't get close enough to the stove and yet I was burning up with fever. . . . I coughed and spat up . . . I think there was blood mixed with the stuff . . . it was frothy and resembled brick dust."[11]

Two doctors, including Jessie's uncle from Mitchell, H. L., corroborated her story, but a special pension hearing examiner countered with his own affidavit, noting, "I found Jessie to be a bright, sprightly young lady . . . while I was there she played the piano, brought in coal twice from another room and fixed the fire . . . she sings in church, helps her auntie do the washing and ironing . . . and she has a regular beau. I never heard her cough once, neither did I see her expectorate. She is a smart, intelligent girl and very much of a lady."[12]

On December 17, 1907, the Pension Bureau rejected Jessie's petition and three months later rejected her appeal, saying "Jessie May Kimberlin is not insane, idiotic, or otherwise permanently helpless."[13] The Pension Bureau was proved right. Jessie, the only daughter of Isaac Kimberlin, married Perry Bussey of Oregon Township, Clark County, Indiana, in 1909, and took into her home her aunt, Mary Abbott, who had vouched for her disability. The marriage produced three children: Carolyn (1911), Edid (1919), and Willima Lee (1922). Jessie lived in Clark County until her death on December 22, 1965. Isaac N. Kimberlin's name disappeared but his line continued well into the mid-twentieth century.

Confused Cousins

It was not unusual for brothers, fathers, and cousins to go off to war side by side. It may be unique, however, for two men with the exact same name and common familial heritage to fight in the same war, return to the same town, share the fate of being crippled by an automobile, and jointly cause confusion on the floor of the U.S. Senate, without knowing each other existed. That is what happened to James H. Kimberlin, times two.

When James H. Kimberlin was mustered out of service at Montgomery, Alabama, on September 10, 1865, he completed an odyssey that saw him serve in four separate regiments—the Fifty-fourth Indiana, the 137th Indiana, the Fiftieth Indiana, and the Fifty-second Indiana. He saw action at Port Gibson, Raymond, and Vicksburg near his cousins in the Twenty-third Indiana, and he saw inaction as a railroad guard in Tennessee and Alabama, and on garrison duty in Alabama. His letters home spoke mostly of camp life as evidenced by his March 1, 1864, note to his uncle Jacob "R" Kimberlin, the same Jacob "R" that the Kimberlins of the Twenty-third Indiana and the Sixty-sixth Indiana wrote to regularly:

> I am not on the land among the living for we are stationed here on an Island about 1 miles square which the Boys calls Hells Half Acr. . . . O Jake you ought to see me go to the gulf and Rake out the oysters I can eat more oysters than any person in Old Scott [county] we are within tenty five miles of mobile where I expect to have to go soon and then Ill get to try my Courage the word is that they are going to shell mobile this evening at 3pm. . . . Tom Clegg is making tea for supper and frying Sunabitch maybe you would have me explain myself what we call Sunofabitch is hardtack mashed up and sweetened and then fried . . . give my love to mother Johnson and my Squires girl tell aunt Bet that I have wished for some of her good corn Bread and potatoes and all the rest of the nix nax. . . . Direct mail to J.H.K. at 50 2nd IN Care Lieut flinn Here is a secesh letter for you to read.[14]

The blue-eyed blonde's military experience, however, was not nearly as eventful as his postwar life. The Lexington, Indiana, native farmed prior to the war, but decided shortly upon his return to settle in Indianapolis, the city of unlimited opportunity for a twenty year old who had survived his service with the nagging effects of scurvy, but no crippling wounds. James H. worked as a shipping clerk in a farm equipment fac-

Merrill Moores served in Congress from March 4, 1915, until March 3, 1925. A lawyer, he also served as Indiana's assistant attorney general from 1894 to 1903.

tory, moving from house to house within Indianapolis. He married Sophia "Nettie" Silvers in that city on August 8, 1878, or 1879,[15] and moved to the Cleveland Block. For some unknown reason, he listed himself in the 1880 census as "Hans Kimberlin" instead of James H.[16] Nevertheless, his occupation and spouse remained the same. They were joined around this time by a sixteen-year-old relative, Nora Kimberlin, who may have done housework to pay for her board.

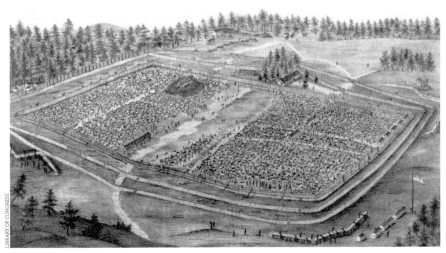

A bird's-eye view of the notorious Andersonville Prison, with prisoners' tents, gallows for executions, and a stream for washing, surrounded by three rows of stockade fences and with artillery batteries of cannons at the corners.

James H. and Nettie moved to 316 West Vermont Street. That is where he was living in 1891 when he filed his first application for a pension, claiming the scurvy and later development of "heart trouble." We know that the couple had no children and that he earned enough money as a shipping clerk to list a twenty-eight-year-old unmarried house servant named Mamie Headley living under the same roof.[17]

The turn of the century began poorly for the Kimberlins and grew steadily worse. Nettie died in 1903 of unknown causes at the age of forty-five. James H. moved to a boardinghouse at 136 West New York Street and at some point switched jobs. He was listed in the 1910 census as being an "inspector of streets and sidewalks," a patronage job like those that many Kimberlins had held off and on since the 1820s.[18] During these years James H. frequently filed for increases in his pension. His application became more earnest in 1913 after he was "crushed" by a car on an Indianapolis street.[19] No details are known but there was no workers compensation back then. He contacted his representatives in Congress, particularly Congressman Merrill Moores and Senator John W. Kern, for intervention.

Photograph shows the overloaded steamboat Sultana *in Helena, Arkansas, on the Mississippi River the day before its boilers exploded and it sank on April 27, 1865.*

At the exact same time James H. was pleading with his congressmen for help, another James H. Kimberlin (hereafter called James Harvey) was sending notes to Washington, D.C., asking about the status of his request for a Civil War pension increase. James Harvey had served as a sergeant in the 124th Indiana beginning with his enlistment on November 30, 1863, in Indianapolis. The 124th Indiana participated in the battle of Atlanta, taking the brunt of Confederate General William J. Hardee's counterattack on July 22, 1864. James Harvey's Company C joined the chase of John Bell Hood's army through Georgia and Alabama until they reached Gaylesville, Alabama, in late October 1864. It was then off by rail to Nashville, where they became part of General George Thomas's Twenty-Third Corps. On November 10, 1864, the 124th Indiana again boarded trains headed for Thompson's Station where they marched toward Pulaski, Tennessee.

Hood was headed for Nashville in an attempt once again to capture a major state capital in Union hands. When Thomas ordered the 124th and its sister regiments to fall back toward Franklin in defense of Nashville, some units were surprised by Confederate cavalry. On November 30, 1864, during heavy skirmishing, all forty members of Company C were

A wood engraving showing the aftermath of the Sultana *disaster that killed numerous former Union prisoners of war released from Andersonville.*

captured at Spring Hill. James Harvey missed the ensuing battle of Franklin, Tennessee. He was on his way to the infamous Confederate prison at Andersonville, Georgia.[20]

The Confederate prison camp at Andersonville was established in February 1864 to house a glut of Union prisoners that had grown exponentially "since prisoner exchanges had virtually ceased during the summer of 1863."[21] Prisoners suffered greater privations in camp than they ever suffered in the field. A lack of replacement clothing, improper medical care, and unsanitary living conditions contributed to a death rate in 1864 of ninety to 130 prisoners each day.[22] In just eight months at Andersonville, more than 10,000 Union prisoners died from gangrene, dysentery, typhoid, and other diseases—a third of the prison population.[23]

In late March 1865 Confederate prison officials began loading thousands of men, described by James Harvey's friend, Lieutenant Joseph Taylor Elliott of the 124th Indiana, as "nothing but skin and bones,"[24] into boxcars for the long ride to Jackson, Mississippi. From there they walked to Vicksburg for final parole. James Harvey was among the 5,500 former prisoners waiting for river transportation at Camp Fisk, four miles from Vicksburg, on April 9, 1865, when General Robert E. Lee surrendered his army to General Ulysses S. Grant at Appomattox Court House.

James Harvey joined 459 fellow Hoosier troops and approximately 2,000 other former prisoners on the decks of the side-wheeler *Sultana* as it pulled away from the Vicksburg wharf at 9:00 p.m. on April 24, 1865. Two days and six hours later, just upriver from Memphis near Paddy's Hens and Chickens Islands, the greatest maritime disaster in American history occurred. A patched boiler blew, setting the wooden packet ship ablaze, throwing hundreds of men into open coal fires, and most of the rest overboard with scalding steam burns. James Harvey was on the hurricane deck and recalled what happened: "the force of the explosion was so great that the boilers were thrown to the east, . . . leaving a great mass of burning coal exposed. . . . those who were unable to extricate themselves were soon burned to death. Others became suddenly crazed . . . lost all sense of reason and power to act . . . were crying, some singing, some praying while others were cursing."[25]

Those on the upper decks jumped from as high as twenty-five feet into the cold water below, right on top of hundreds of struggling soldiers too weak from their prison experience to hold on for long. James Harvey described the bedlam: "the poor, crazed fellows never paused to look, having wrenched a door or a window shutter from its fastenings. . . . others had secured sticks of wood, a plank, a scantling . . . anything that might act as a float. . . . when I looked out over the water where but a few minutes before there were hundreds of men struggling for supremacy, now there were but few to be seen. The great mass of them had gone down, clinging to each other."[26] Those who made it away from the boat had a long swim. The *Sultana* was 300 yards from the eastern shore and 1,800 yards from the Arkansas shore. James Harvey jumped off the west side of the boat with a plank for a float and was picked up by rowboats lowered by the steamer *Bostana*. An estimated 1,800 of his fellow soldiers never made it to shore.

James Harvey was mustered out of service at Indianapolis on May 16, 1865, and stayed in the area, moving between Indianapolis, Lawrence, Allisonville, Castleton, and eventually settling in McCordsville, Indiana. He farmed near Castleton until 1874. The 1880 census showed James Harvey living in McCordsville with his wife of twelve years, Lucy (Church) Kimberlin, and five children. He supported his family by working as a carpenter.[27] Two more children were born in the early 1880s.

James Harvey's lingering wartime maladies caught up with him in the mid-1880s. Claiming "disease of the rectum and rheumatism," he applied for a pension based on his two years of service.[28] He spent the next thirty-nine years in a never-ending campaign to have that meager pension increased. In 1882 James Harvey switched jobs. He became a mail clerk for the railroad and frequently stayed at the National Hotel in downtown Indianapolis the night before a trip to outlying towns.

On election day, November 3, 1886, he checked into Room 37 at the National before lighting a cigar and walking with a friend to the state Republican headquarters at Market and Pennsylvania Streets to watch as election returns came in. According to a handwritten affidavit James Harvey filed with one of his numerous pension petitions, he did not drink to excess that night.[29] Nevertheless, when he returned to his hotel room around midnight he caught his last three hours of good sleep for the rest of his life. According to James Harvey, around 3:00 a.m. he opened the floor-to-ceiling window of his third floor room to step out to relieve himself. He fell nearly thirty feet to an iron grate below, breaking his leg and back in the fall. He was put on a stretcher and taken by rail to McCordsville and examined later that day by his second cousin, Doctor Albert Kimberlin. He was fitted with a stiff leather back brace that he wore for the rest of his life, always uncomfortable and in pain.

James Harvey told a skeptical pension review board years later that he "had dreamed I was staying on the ground floor of another hotel that I frequented, where the floor to ceiling windows opened to a lawn where I could relieve myself."[30] Instead, he awoke "hanging by my fingers from a sill until I could no longer hang on."[31] The pension board declined his petition for a pension increase, but James Harvey did not give up his campaign. He applied again in 1902 and was examined by a doctor. The medical examiner described him as "an intelligent man, and he has occupied positions of responsibility . . . has been somewhat of a politician."[32]

By the turn of the century, James Harvey had moved his family to nearby Vernon, Indiana, and was working as a "lumber dealer." Only seventeen-year-old Elmer and twenty-one- year-old Homer, a pharmacist, remained at home. Nineteen-year-old William is listed as being "at school."[33] Another job change during the next ten years brought James Harvey back to downtown Indianapolis as a "watchman at the Soldiers and Sailors Monument."[34] By 1910 it is obvious that he and his wife's

U.S. Senator John W. Kern of Indiana. In 1908 he ran as vice president with Demo-cratic presidential candidate William Jennings Bryan, who lost to Republican William Howard Taft.

prospects (possibly health related) had dimmed. His twenty-nine-year-old son, William, himself a mail carrier, and William's twenty-year-old wife, Lyda moved in with the older generation, though James Harvey was still listed as "head of household."[35]

Age and more bad luck did not seem to slow James Harvey down. He continued his one-man campaign for a pension increase, writing several letters to Senator Kern. Meanwhile, his right "good leg" was broken above the knee when he was run over by a car in downtown Indianapolis, and his wife of forty-six years died in 1914.

In 1916 Kern filed a private bill setting James H. Kimberlin's pension at thirty-six dollars per month. The bill passed August 22, 1916, and President William Howard Taft signed the bill September 5, 1916. You would think that would mark a final victory for James Harvey, but the confusion was just beginning. Kern sent James Harvey a letter informing him of his success. However, the increase was not reflected on his next pension check. By October 1916 he fired off letters to the pension office in Washington demanding to know why he was not receiving his increase.[36]

Meanwhile, the other James "H" in our story was also demanding to know why his pension had not been increased. Both James Harvey and James H. believed that Kern had been working on their behalf. A chance meeting of the two men in Indianapolis on October 12, 1916, solved the mystery that no government bureaucrat could decipher. James H. described the meeting in a clarifying letter written later that same day: "I met a man to day who lives at McCordsville, Ind, and I asked him if he had ever filed papers for a special bill in his behalf. He said that he had not, then he pulled a letter from his pocket from Senator Kern saying that his bill had passed both houses and signed by the president and was now law. He spells his name the same as I, James H. Kimberlin!"[37] James H. Kimberlin and James Harvey Kimberlin had both lived in the same area for almost fifty years, had both been run over by automobiles in the same town, were both Civil War pensioners, and if not for chance, would never have met nor discovered that they were second cousins.

Although both had filed for pension increases, the Kern bill had been submitted on behalf of James H. It was Kern who had mistakenly sent the good pension news to James Harvey.[38] James H., with his newly increased pension, lived as a retired clerk, at some point taking in his older sister Mary E. Daly.[39] He died in Indianapolis in 1925. James Harvey continued his campaign for a pension increase. In 1923 his son, Homer, filed an affidavit on his father's behalf, saying that James Harvey had "prostate and kidney trouble."[40] A medical examiner's report filed that same year described James Harvey as "senile and suffering from arteriosclerosis."[41] Still, on October 1, 1923, James Harvey had enough presence of mind to write to U.S. Senator James Watson, greeting him as "Friend Jim."[42] In the letter James Harvey complained that as a notary public, he had filed for himself and others more than fifty pension increase petitions, and although he is grateful that his last pension increase petition of August 1922 was approved, it should have been effective from the date of application. He wrote: "I do not think I will allow my case to rest at this; I think I shall take an appointment to the Sect of the Interior. I know my increase should date from the date of filing." It is unknown if James Harvey's last appeal would have been successful. Before it could be resolved, he died in McCordsville on April 28, 1924.

James Harvey was a man of pluck, resourcefulness, and a good deal of luck. He survived Andersonville when 12,000 comrades did not. He survived the *Sultana* when nearly 1,800 others did not. He survived a thirty-foot fall when not too many others would have survived. Given his record, odds are he would have browbeaten the secretary of the interior into submission, too.

Drunk and Ill-Tempered

Not all Kimberlins, nor all veterans for that matter, were able to build productive postwar lives. Some returned home to broken marriages, others suffered from what we now recognize as posttraumatic stress disorder, and many found it difficult to settle down to the more mundane life of father, husband, and farmer.

Henry Kimberlin was one of the last young Kimberlins to sign up for the Union cause. He was the fifth of twelve children of James Washington and Permelia "Millie" Smith Kimberlin. His brothers, John B. and Abraham, had preceded him to war. Henry was enrolled in Company D of the Forty-ninth Indiana on August 13, 1864, by a Lieutenant Hamacher. The eighteen-year-old Henry was tall for a Kimberlin at five feet, eleven inches and had black eyes and dark hair. Like most of his relatives, he was a farmer.[43]

The Forty-ninth Indiana was a veteran unit, having fought alongside the Twenty-third Indiana in Grant's Vicksburg campaign and in all the battles from Port Gibson through the siege of Vicksburg. When Henry enlisted, the Forty-ninth was home on a veterans' leave. He may have replaced a local Scott County veteran whose term was up. Henry never saw battle. As soon as his unit arrived in Indianapolis following leave, they were sent to Lexington, Kentucky, for garrison duty until the end of the war. Henry was discharged in July 1865, eight weeks before the Forty-ninth Indiana disbanded for good.

Upon returning home, Henry fit right back into the business of the family farm. The 1870 census sheet that listed him as a laborer living with his parents and four siblings was signed by census taker James Powers on June 10, 1870, the same day Henry married Eliza (aka Louisa) Righthouse.[44] Henry and Eliza may have had a rough start. Both were illiterate, which limited their economic prospects. They also may have had their first son, Andrew Jefferson, before they were married. The record is contradictory. In his application for a Civil War pension, Henry stated that Andrew Jefferson was born in April 1870.[45] The 1880 census, however, listed Andrew Jefferson as being eight years old, which puts his birth date in 1872.[46] Eventually, Henry and Eliza had ten children. Henry received his pension in 1890 after claiming varicose veins, rheumatism, piles, and deafness in his left ear.[47]

We do not know what Henry's economic or family circumstances were in 1890, as the census for that year was destroyed by a fire in 1921. Only fragments remain. In fact, after the 1880 census, Henry disappears from future censuses. He shows up again, however, because of his marriage problems. In October 1905 Eliza claimed Henry beat and abandoned her. She filed a petition to gain one-half of Henry's pension, saying, "for several years usually about the time he would receive his pension check he would get drunk and come home and abuse her . . . and many times he would drive them out of the house and they would have to stay of nights with neighbors. . . . at last on the 14th day of August, 1905, he came home drunk and threatened to kill her."[48] She said he was a drunk and ill-tempered; he said she was unfaithful and a poor housekeeper. Henry counter-filed with the Pension Bureau on July 20, 1906, saying, "I hereby agree to give Liza Kimbelin one-half of my pension $18 dollars commencing August 4, 1906. This is exactly what I agreed to do when she ordered me out. You do this and I accept it. There is another law that will make me free."[49] Henry was found dead along a railroad track near Charlestown, Indiana, on May 6, 1908. Eliza filed for a widow's pension that same year and lived in Nabb, Indiana, until her death in 1926. Henry and Eliza never divorced.

Kimberlin Through and Through

Scott County society in the 1830s was still fairly isolated. At this time Abraham Kimberlin ran a general store and tannery near Nabb, Indiana. His was one of six general stores in Scott County. The Kimberlin ledger documents family members working together and selling each other finished goods. In that part of the county, if you were not a Kimberlin there was a good chance you were related to one.

In that close environment it is not surprising that a Kimberlin married a Kimberlin. That is what happened on February 24, 1838, when Abraham's son, William Henry Harrison Kimberlin, married his first cousin, Elizabeth (Betsy) Kimberlin. Betsy was from the line of Daniel Kimberlin, the veteran of the War of 1812, and the first person married (to Ursula Brinton) in what became Scott County. Betsy had previously been married to another cousin, William Whitlach (1831).[50] William "H" and Betsy had three children, including Abraham (a popular Kimberlin name), Martha, and Catherine (or Kate). William H. left Betsy in 1844 for unknown reasons and never returned. For the next eight years she raised the children alone and finally divorced her husband in March 1852.[51] He died in the state insane asylum in Indianapolis in 1853.

Young Abraham Kimberlin (he was also listed as Abram from time to time) was an explorer. In 1860, at age nineteen, he lived for a time in Lykins, Kansas. The 1860 census does not assign him an occupation. His purpose there is not recorded. He lived in a household of persons from Connecticut and New York, possibly as a boarder.[52] Nevertheless, he returned to Scott County in time to enlist in Company D, Thirty-eighth Indiana, on August 24, 1861. The regiment moved to Louisville, Kentucky, then on to Green River and Bowling Green, Kentucky. At Green River, Abraham apparently ate green apples and field corn, getting very sick by the time he camped at Hartsville. He later reported: "I would have a drink of water and it would pass through me before I could get my pants down."[53] The bowel trouble never left Abraham and the army sent him to General Hospital Number 1 in Louisville for treatment, then gave him a fifty-day leave to go home for his mother's cooking. He returned to the hospital in Louisville and stayed there until his medical discharge on June 20, 1862. When Abraham came home the second time, he resumed his work as a farmer near New Philadelphia in Scott County.

War talk, and undoubtedly the well-documented exchange of letters with cousins on the battlefield, inspired Abraham to enlist a second time, February 10, 1864, after a two-year break. This time it was with Company E, Thirteenth Indiana Cavalry.[54] "They were excited around there [Scott County] about the call for more soldiers in 1864, and I enlisted again thinking I could stand it," he said.[55]

The Thirteenth Indiana moved to Nashville, Tennessee, then on to Huntsville, Alabama, where it helped to repulse a Confederate attack on Huntsville in late October 1864. Company E was then detached with several other companies and participated in the siege of Decatur, Alabama, in October 1864, and the battle of Franklin, Tennessee, in December, where, Abraham said. "I lost my boots."[56] His chronic diarrhea plagued him throughout 1864. Abraham was a patient at the Zollicatter House in Nashville, where he complained there were no cots. He was hospitalized again in Shreveport, Louisiana. In fact, when he says he "participated in the battle at Franklin," he may have been exaggerating. His fellow soldiers remembered him years later simply as the company bugler who was always sick. John Norrington of Floyd's Knobs said, "Whenever sick call was made, the boys would say 'there goes Abe to the doctor.'"[57] Another comrade, Thomas Mull of Chestnut Hill, said he never saw Abraham in battle.

Abraham was able to travel with his company to Vicksburg in the winter of 1864 and back to New Orleans and Mobile, Alabama, where he participated in the capture of that city on April 12, 1865. By then he was sick again. Another stay in the military hospital at Mobile from April to August 22, 1865, led to his medical discharge, while the rest of his company performed garrison duty in Vicksburg.

Abraham returned to Scott County and resumed his farm work, but not for long. He moved to Illinois in 1868, and went to work for his uncle, F. M. "Marion" Kimberlin, in Carthage, Missouri, for awhile. "He came to work for me in 1869," said Marion. "I know because that was the year of the total eclipse of the Sun."[58] Abraham returned to Illinois long enough to court a young lady, Perlina "Ellen" Dukes, who was a chambermaid in Charles Tewskbury's Inn at Tolono, Illinois.[59] They were married on August 6, 1873, in Scott County. The couple is also recorded as being married in October 1873 in Tolono. The couple settled in Hoopeston, Illinois, where the 1880 census recorded Abraham as being a "drayman" with three children.[60] They had two more children in the 1880s. We do not know much about their lives between 1880 and 1900 because of the destruction of the 1890 census. We do know that in 1900 they were still living in Hoopeston, Illinois, with their two youngest surviving children, Emma Cecile and Roxanna. Abraham was working as a day laborer.[61] Abraham and Ellen secured some financial stability despite that fact that he was always a laborer or farm hand and she did not work outside the home. The 1920 census lists them as being retired, but owning their own home.[62]

At some point, Abraham's health must have failed, because in 1921, when his petition for an increase in his Civil War pension was denied, he listed his address as "Soldier's Home, Cottage 10, Quincy, Illinois."[63] The 1930 census, however, listed Abraham and Ellen as married in Hoopeston and living in their own home worth $1,000.[64] Abraham gave his address on a pension petition as "Soldier's Home, Lafayette, Indiana."[65] Abraham was discharged from the Soldier's Home in Lafayette just months before his death in 1931. He had survived a lifetime of illness, was married for almost sixty years, and fathered six children.

Politics and Pensions

The death of one Kimberlin clan member, James Starkes, illustrated how Civil War pensions were used to damage lives rather than support them. James was a private in Company I, Twenty-third Indiana, along with many of his Kimberlin cousins, including Benjamin, William H., and Jacob T. James never saw battle. The closest he came to action was a forced march from Paducah to Belmont, Missouri, November 6 to 7, 1861. The regiment marched forty-one hours straight, but never fired a shot.[66] It was boredom that James complained about to his father, Henry Stark, in a letter dated October 17, 1861, shortly after his father had visited him in camp: "We did not get sight of one reble even so much as to smell one much less to see him."[67] Still, James was healthy at this point. "I am well at present time and hope that theas few lines will find you the same," he wrote.[68] James's health did not hold up for long. Within weeks he was in a military hospital at Paducah, with pneumonia; he died on January 18, 1862.

Henry went to Paducah to claim his son's body, then returned to his wife, Louisa, an invalid, and the five surviving children at home in New Albany. Henry had been a tollgate keeper on the New Albany to Paoli Pike since 1833. He worked at the Fredricksburg gate until 1855 at the rate of eight dollars per month, then transferred to New Albany Gate Number 1, where his pay increased to twenty dollars per month.[69] At New Albany, the family lived in or near the tollhouse, in apparently crowded conditions. The 1860 census listed, in addition to Henry's family of eight, twenty-eight persons with the family names of Bartee, Kenneyer, McCoy, Canfield, White, Fan, Dunn, and Lamb, all living in the same household. We do not know if the thirty-six people actually lived in the same home or were tenants in a boardinghouse or simply listed the tollhouse as their address for mail purposes. Nevertheless, Henry supported his family there until July 4, 1865, when he moved them to an eighty-six-acre farm his wife had inherited from her father and located one and one-half miles northeast of Greenville, Indiana. There, Henry relied primarily on cash generated from renting his fields.

Henry's work record and his move to the farm became controversial in the 1880s after he had applied for and secured a Civil War pension based on the premise that James had provided some support for Henry and the rest of the family. In his initial application for a survivor's pension in May 1881, Henry said, "I did not know there was a possible pension until I picked up a newspaper at the post office and saw the picture of a soldier with the words 'Pensions for All.' I went twelve miles to New Albany and saw John O. Neu and he said 'you are a damned fool you did not apply long ago.'"[70]

Henry's pension application was supported by affidavits from friends and employers of James, who swore James turned his money over to his father. John Mitchell, a boyhood friend of James, said he chopped wood with James in 1860 and 1861, and that all wages went to Henry.[71] James also worked at Henry Turner's brickyard from 1854 to 1861. According to Turner, James "gave most of his wages to his father."[72] Further corroboration came in James's own hand from the earlier cited October 17, 1861, letter to Henry: "I want to now whether you got safe home or not and whether you got that mony or not that I sent by Jackson and Sam Roby."[73]

Henry's pension was approved in 1883 at the rate of eight dollars per month, but he did not get to enjoy it for long. John Schamuel wrote the U.S. Commissioner of Pensions on December 31, 1886, "I believe we have a fraudulent pensioner in our vicinity."[74] James Stark, according to Schamuel, "went to war because he was driven off from home."[75] A series of affidavits and counteraffidavits flew to the pension office in Washington, DC, each claiming to know the truth about Henry's financial need. Samuel Miller swore that Henry "left the toll gate because his wife said he was spending his money on prostitutes and she had to get him away from there."[76]

Family came to Henry's defense. His two eldest daughters, Mary Rankin and Emeline Fawkes, confirmed that their father had never made more than twenty-five dollars per month through 1863 (his detractors had claimed it was forty dollars), and Jacob Sheets (he and Henry had married sisters) said Henry could not have afforded the farm if it had not been inherited.[77]

Finally, Henry came to his own defense. In a letter to the pension commissioner, Henry said the testimony of Peter, Sarah, and John Schamuel was "with malice, because I pointed John out to a City Marshall who held a warrant for his arrest."[78] As for Samuel Miller, "he testified against me because I am a Republican."[79]

Henry's pension was suspended in August 1887, but was reinstated in 1889 after he filed a petition for recertification. His enemies had forgotten about him, and pension officials soon did, too. Henry died on December 19, 1893. He was receiving thirty-six dollars per month, more than he ever made as a tollgate keeper, when he died.

Scattered to the Winds

The stories of Isaac Newton; James H., James Harvey, Henry, and Abraham Kimberlin; and Henry Stark offer a perspective on postwar life that would not be markedly different from the lives of the rest of the Kimberlin clan (including the Houghs, Whitlachs, Starks, and Williams) or, for that matter, the Civil War veteran population at large. The veterans married, divorced, fathered large families, worked into old age, and slowly faded into history. They had their share of alcoholism, mental illness, and financial trouble. The surviving generation of Kimberlins did not produce a senator or congressman, a bank president or a general. But they did contribute to the formation of the cultural fabric of the Midwest and beyond as they transplanted their "Old Scott" values to their new homes and applied them to new challenges.

For nearly one hundred years the Civil War affected the lives of the extended Kimberlin family. The pensions earned by the blood and illness

The Kimberlin clan gathers outside of the family's second home in Scott County.

of the Kimberlin soldiers provided some support for widows, parents, children, and grandchildren who had known the war only at a distance, if at all. But stories, the memories, and in many cases the pain, never left them. Ultimately, the thirty-three members of the extended Kimberlin family who enlisted, fought, and sometimes died for the Union, achieved their primary goal: To secure the Union and the way of life that promised equal opportunity to all, to succeed or fail.

Conclusion

Frank Klement, in *Lincoln's Critics: The Copperheads of the North,* quoted Napoleon as saying, "History is a myth men agree to believe."[80] If that is so, then what are we to believe about Copperheadism and the Kimberlin family's actions during the Civil War? We have no record of how the Kimberlins felt on June 12, 1865, as the Twenty-third Indiana and the Sixty-sixth Indiana were honored in a ceremony on the statehouse grounds in Indianapolis.[81] Their many letters to and from the battlefield never described themselves as "patriots." Given the evidence of significant Copperhead sentiment and actions in Scott County and nearby counties

Top: Historical marker for the John Kimberlin farm in Scott County. *Above:* Graves of John Kimberlin and his wife, Ruth Jones Kimberlin.

during the war, however, one can conclude that by sending thirty-three family members to fight for the Union, the Kimberlins certainly took risks both on the battlefield and at home that many if not most of their southern Indiana neighbors were unwilling to take.

One can argue that the Kimberlins, possibly more than any family in their area, understood and appreciated that the land they lived on and the principles upon which Scott County was founded, were worth preserving. After all, it was the Kimberlins who first took the risk of moving into what had been "Indian" country to work for their dream of a free existence, independent even of the societal ties that existed nearby in Louisville. It is not too corny to suggest that the Kimberlin family record of fighting at Tippecanoe, starting one of the first commercial ventures in Scott County, and becoming one of the more substantial extended families in southern Indiana reinforced and nurtured their collective pride in what had become of their county and their country.

When war broke out, thousands of patriotic Hoosiers flocked to the enlistment stations across Indiana. The Kimberlins' fervor, however, lasted well beyond the initial rush of patriotism. The Kimberlins marched down the Charlestown Road to war more than a year before the draft, and they and their cousins continued to enlist, even when Copperheadism reared its head. In fact, the author has found no evidence that any Kimberlin family member chose not to reenlist when the opportunity presented itself. The evidence is quite the opposite. Only "young" Abraham Kimberlin and James H. Kimberlin came home after their initial enlistments expired, and they both reenlisted at a later time.

We have only one letter from the home front in Scott County to the battlefield that survived the rain and mud and unlikely return path to be read and understood today. That is a letter from "old" Isaac to his son, Jacob R. Kimberlin, upon the formation of the Sixty-sixth Indiana. There must have been, however, hundreds of such letters telling of the Copperhead rallies, the violence brought down upon the heads of draft officers, and the family and societal turmoil stoked by those who thought fighting for African Americans was distasteful at best, unpatriotic at worst. When diaries like those of Sarah Waldschmidt Young Bovard and newspaper accounts of "secesh" meetings reached the Kimberlins, they did not equivocate like many of their famous neighbors, William English, James Cravens, Horace Heffren, and Jesse Bright did. They stuck with their duty even when they had a chance to come home. Most of the Kimberlins could have come home with honor by mid-1864, banged-up and sick as many of them were. Yet, only those who were dead or chronically ill did not stick with their units until the grand parades in June 1865.

The overriding sentiment of the Kimberlins and their cousins who went to war may best have been summed up by John J. Kimberlin, writing from camp at Lake Providence, Louisiana, on April 12, 1863. In obvious response to news from home, John J. bristled and fired back that "we will show our old copperheads at home that our old flag shall not be insulted."[82]

Were the Kimberlins patriots? The evidence certainly suggests so. By Scott County standards the answer would again be yes. Only one family member, Isaac Newton Kimberlin, was recognized as an official hero. However, the Kimberlins' attention to duty and their steadfastness under extreme conditions was also heroic, even though they would never have thought themselves so.

Ultimately, the Kimberlins were caught up in seismic changes in culture, politics, and economics that disrupted their way of life and forced upon them life-and-death decisions that have reverberated for generations. In the course of just three generations of Kimberlins, the subsistence economy of the frontier became a bustling, railroad-based, market economy. Man-to-man politics of the homestead evolved into rough-and-tumble party campaigns with national consequences. The clash of the slave culture with the worldwide movement for human rights, resulting in the Civil War, caused each Kimberlin to weigh in his or her mind some of the greatest questions of any age.

In the end, the Kimberlins changed their local economy, played a role in their political world, and, it can be argued, contributed more than their share to the victory of freedom over slavery. Yet, despite all of the upheaval they endured, despite personal sacrifice on a scale unmatched in their little world, the Kimberlins' core beliefs remained true. From their letters in a new land, to their battlefield accounts, to their attempts to secure a stable economic legacy for their descendants, the surviving written record shows that they were simply trying to preserve a lifestyle that they had helped create sixty years earlier when John Kimberlin first settled along the creek that eventually bore his name.

Notes

Chapter 1

1. *A Chronology of Indiana in the Civil War* (Indianapolis: Indiana Civil War Centennial Commission, 1965), 8.

2. Carl Bogardus, *The Centennial History of Austin, Scott County, Indiana* (Paoli, IN: Historical Committee of the Centennial Celebration, 1953), 78.

3. Muster Rolls of Indiana Civil War Volunteers, Indiana State Archives, Indianapolis, IN (hereafter cited as Muster Rolls). The Stark family name has also been spelled Starkes.

4. *Lexington: A Pioneer Town* (Scottsburg, IN: Lexington Historical Society, 1988), 69.

5. Muster Rolls.

6. Ruth Crim, "History of the Kimberlin Family of Virginia, Kentucky, and Indiana," Historical Marker File #72.2001.02, Indiana Historical Bureau, Indianapolis, IN.

7. Clark's Grant Board of Commissioners (VA), "Proceedings, 1783–1846," typescript, 57, William Henry Smith Memorial Library, Indiana Historical Society, Indianapolis, IN.

8. Deed Record A-240, Indiana, Recorder's Office, Jefferson County, IN.

9. Carl Bogardus, *Pioneer Life in Scott County* (Austin, IN: Muscatatuck Press, 1957), 4.

10. Crim, "History of the Kimberlin Family of Virginia, Kentucky, and Indiana."

11. Carl Bogardus, *Early History of Scott County, 1820–1870* (Scottsburg, IN: Scott County Historical Society, 1970), 7.

12. Ibid., 15.

13. Lizzie D. Coleman, *History of the Pigeon Roost Massacre* (Mitchell, IN: Commercial Print, 1904).

14. Declaration of Soldier for Pension, War of 1812, Record Group 15A-SO 10690, National Archives, Washington, DC.

15. "Gibson's Message to Colonel Hargrove," in *Messages and Letters of William Henry Harrison*, Logan Esarey, ed., Indiana Historical Collections, vol. 9 (Indianapolis: Indiana Historical Commission, 1922), 70–71.

16. Memorial to Congress by Citizens of Clark County, HF: 12 Cong., 2 sess: DS, October 15, 1812, *Congressional Record*.

17. Record Group 217, Records of the General Accounting Office, File 1773/34, National Archives.

18. J. Thompson, third auditor, Treasury Department, 1834, ibid.

19. Bogardus, *Early History of Scott County*, 7.

20. Mary Wilson and Ann Asher, "Lexington" pamphlet, 88, Manuscript Collection, Indiana Historical Society.

21. Ibid., 37.

22. Arville Funk, *Hoosiers in the Civil War* (Chicago: Adams Press, 1967), 58.

23. Jacob Piatt Dunn Jr., *Indiana and Indianans*, 5 vols. (Chicago: American Historical Society, 1919), 2:608–9.

24. Muster Rolls.

25. John J. Hardin letter, July 21, 1861, John J. Hardin Papers, MS174, Collection L209, Indiana State Library, Indianapolis, IN.

26. Ibid.

27. *Chronology of Indiana in the Civil War*, 12.

28. John J. Kimberlin to Jacob R. Kimberlin, September 24, 1861, Kimberlin Family Papers, private collection (hereafter cited as Kimberlin Papers).

29. William and Benjamin Kimberlin to Jacob R. Kimberlin, November 10, 1861, Kimberlin Papers.

30. James Stark to Jacob R. Kimberlin, December 1861, ibid.

31. Stark to Jacob R. Kimberlin, December 25, 1861, ibid.

32. April 13, 1861, Sarah Waldschmidt Young Bovard Diary, Ancestry.com (hereafter cited as Bovard Diary).

33. John David Barnhart, *The Impact of the Civil War on Indiana* (Indianapolis: Indiana Civil War Centennial Commission, 1962), 10.

34. Lorna Lutes Sylvester, "Oliver P. Morton and Hoosier Politics during the Civil War" (PhD diss., Indiana University, 1968), 48.

35. July 28, 1861, Bovard Diary.

36. September 22, 1861, ibid.

37. September 24, 1861, ibid.

38. November 21, 1861, ibid.

39. Emma Lou Thornbrough, *Indiana in the Civil War Era, 1850–1880* (Indianapolis: Indiana Historical Society, 1989), 181.

40. Marjorie Perry, "Opposition to the Civil War in Indiana" (MA thesis, University of Washington, 1931), 2.

41. Frank Klement, *Copperheads in the Middle West* (Chicago: University of Chicago Press, 1960), 32.

42. William G. Edison, with Vincent Akers, "Attitudes in Johnson County during the Civil War: The Demaree Papers," *Indiana Magazine of History* 70 (March, 1974): 64.

43. Alt Perring, letter, April, 20, 1864, Alderice Family Papers, MS124, Collection L209, Guide to the Indiana Sesquicentennial Manuscript Project: Part 1, Indiana State Library.

44. Barnhart, *Impact of the Civil War on Indiana*, 11.

Chapter 2

1. Maggie Henretty, "A History of Scott County" (typed manuscript in the Indiana State Library), chapter 12.

2. Ibid.

3. Ibid.

4. William Thorndale and William Dollanhide, *Map Guide to the U.S. Federal Censuses, 1790–1920* (Baltimore, MD: Genealogical Publishing Company, 1987), 106.

5. James H. Madison, *The Indiana Way* (Bloomington: Indiana University Press, 1986), 37.

6. Thorndale and Dollanhide, *Map Guide to the U.S. Federal Censuses*, 107.

7. Tench Coxe, "District of Indiana," in *Book 2 of the Third Census of the United States, 1810: A Statement of the Arts and Manufactures of the United States for the Year 1810* (Philadelphia: A. Cornman, 1814).

8. Madison, *Indiana Way*, 50.

9. Carl Bogardus, *The Centennial History of Austin, Scott County, Indiana* (Paoli, IN: Historical Committee of the Centennial Celebration, 1953), 12.

10. Ibid., 87.

11. Ibid., 7.

12. Ibid.

13. Ibid., 7–8.

14. Madison, *Indiana Way*, 63–64.

15. Carl Bogardus, *Early History of Scott County, 1820–1870* (Scottsburg, IN: Scott County Historical Society, 1970), 21.

16. John Long, ed., *Atlas of Historical County Boundaries* (New York: Charles Scribner and Sons, 1996), 272.

17. 1820 US Census.

18. Ibid.

19. Ibid.

20. United States Census Office, *Digest of Accounts of Manufacturing Establishments in the United States, and Their Manufactures, Made under Direction of the Secretary of State, in Pursuance of a Resolution of Congress, of 30th March, 1822* (Washington, DC: Gales and Seaton, 1823).

21. Ibid.

22. Ibid.

23. Madison, *Indiana Way*, 87.

24. Abraham Kimberlin Business Ledger, private collection. The material in the following six paragraphs is drawn from this source.

25. Madison, *Indiana Way*, 75.

26. *Statistics of the United States of America, as Collected and Returned by the Marshals of the Several Judicial Districts under the Thirteenth Section of the Act for Taking the Sixth Census Corrected at the Department of State* (Washington: Blair and Rives, 1842), 337.

27. Ibid.

28. Ibid., 336

29. Ibid.

30. Madison, *Indiana Way*, 80–81.

31. Ibid., 95.

32. Bogardus, *Early History of Scott County*, 27.

33. Ibid.

34. 1850 US Census.

35. Ibid.

36. Ibid.

37. Charles Keyser, *The Life of William H. English* (Philadelphia, PA: Ferguson Brothers, 1880).

38. Scott County Order Book B2, 1823–1826, Scott County Historical Society, Scottsburg, IN.

39. Keyser, *Life of William H. English*.

40. Ibid.

41. Ibid.

42. 1860 US Census.

43. Ibid.

44. *Lexington Clipper*, September 23, 1858.

45. 1860 US Census.

46. Walter Dean Burnham, *Presidential Ballots, 1836–1892* (Baltimore, MD: Johns Hopkins University Press, 1955), 406.

47. Frank Klement, *The Copperheads in the Middle West* (Chicago: University of Chicago Press, 1960), 3.

48. Ibid., 4.

49. Ibid., 6.

50. Ibid., 9.

51. Kenneth Stampp, "The Impact of the Civil War upon Hoosier Society," *Indiana Magazine of History* 38 (March 1942): 5.

52. Undated letter to Oliver Morton, cited in "New Indiana Archival Documents," *Indiana Magazine of History* 32 (December 1936): 363.

53. *New Albany Weekly Ledger*, November, 28, 1860.

54. Lorna Lutes Sylvester, "Oliver P. Morton and Hoosier Politics during the Civil War" (PhD diss., Indiana University, 1968), 45.

55. Ibid., 109.

Chapter 3

1. Dorothy Riker and Gayle Thornbrough, eds., *Indiana Election Returns, 1816–1851* (Indianapolis: Indiana Historical Bureau, 1960), x.

2. Carl Bogardus, *The Centennial History of Austin, Scott County, Indiana* (Paoli, IN: Historical Committee of the Centennial Celebration, 1953), 5.

3. Riker and Thornbrough, eds., *Indiana Election Returns*, 137.

4. Ibid., 71.

5. Ibid., 138–39.

6. Scott County Order Book Number 1, 1820–1823, First Circuit Court, 1820 November Term, First Day, Scott County Historical Society, Scottsburg, IN.

7. Riker and Thornbrough, eds., *Indiana Election Returns*, 4–9.

8. Ibid.

9. Emma Lou Thornbrough, *Indiana in the Civil War Era, 1850–1880* (Indianapolis: Indiana Historical Bureau and Indiana Historical Society, 1989), 1.

10. Logan Esarey, "Pioneer Politics in Indiana," *Indiana Magazine of History* 13 (June 1917): 104–5.

11. Voting poll books and tally sheets, Scott County Historical Center, Genealogy Division, Scottsburg, IN. Results for some elections are missing. The condition of the original documents varies greatly.

12. Riker and Thornbrough, eds., *Indiana Election Returns*, 139.

13. Esarey, "Pioneer Politics in Indiana," 124.

14. Riker and Thornbrough, eds., *Indiana Election Returns*, 140–41.

15. Ibid., 10–12.

16. Ibid., 85, 86.

17. Ibid., 141–43.

18. Ibid., 14–19.

19. Ibid., 87–90.

20. Ibid., xxx.

21. Esarey, "Pioneer Politics in Indiana," 125.

22. Ibid., 129.

23. Thornbrough, *Indiana in the Civil War Era*, 13.

24. Ibid.

25. Ibid., 17.

26. Ibid., 3.

27. Phillip Crane, "Onus with Honor: A Political History of Joseph A. Wright, 1809–1857" (MA thesis, Indiana University, 1961), 132–34.

28. Thornbrough, *Indiana in the Civil War Era*, 47.

29. *Madison Courier*, October 23, 1850.

30. State Election Returns, 50-Q, Boxes 20–22, Indiana State Archives, Indianapolis, IN.

31. Justin E. Walsh, *Centennial History of the Indiana General Assembly, 1816–1978* (Indianapolis: The Select Committee on the Centennial History of the Indiana General Assembly, 1987), 15.

32. Thornbrough, *Indiana in the Civil War Era*, 50.

33. Abstract of Votes, Secretary of State Election Returns, Microfilm Roll Number 6617, Indiana State Archives.

34. Election Results for Lexington Township, Scott County, October 1853, and for Scott County, Scott County Historical Society.

35. Charles Keyser, *The Life of William H. English* (Philadelphia, PA: Ferguson Brothers, 1880), 8.

36. Ibid., 12.

37. Kenneth Stampp, *America in 1857: A Nation on the Brink* (New York: Oxford University Press, 1990), 4.

38. Ibid., 5.

39. *Madison Courier*, April 18, 1854.

40. Thornbrough, *Indiana in the Civil War Era*, 60.

41. Ibid., 60–61

42. Abstract of Votes, Secretary of State Election Returns.

43. Carl Fremont Brand, "The History of the Know Nothing Party in Indiana," *Indiana Magazine of History* 18 (March, 1922): 62.

44. Thornbrough, *Indiana in the Civil War Era*, 68.

45. Ibid., 74.

46. Ibid., 71.

47. Roger H. Van Bolt, "The Rise of the Republican Party in Indiana, 1855–1856," *Indiana Magazine of History* 51 (September, 1955): 213.

48. Stampp, *America in 1857*, p. 102.

49. Phillip Klein, *President James Buchannan* (University Park: Pennsylvania State University Press, 1962), 296.

50. Stampp, *America in 1857*, p. 272.

51. Klein, *President James Buchannan*, 300.

52. Ibid., 312.

53. Ibid.

54. Keyser, *Life of William H. English*.

55. F. Gerald Handfieled Jr., "Life of William English," in Ralph Gray, ed., *Gentlemen from Indiana: National Party Candidates, 1836–1940* (Indianapolis, Indiana: Indiana Historical Bureau, 1977), 92.

56. Ibid.

57. Ibid.

58. Keyser, *Life of William H. English.*

59. Thornbrough, *Indiana in the Civil War Era*, 82.

Chapter 4

1. Emma Lou Thornbrough, *Indiana in the Civil War Era, 1850–1880* (Indianapolis: Indiana Historical Bureau, 1989), 86–87.

2. Thomas J. Kelso, "The German-American Vote in the Election of 1860: The Case of Indiana with Supporting Data from Ohio" (PhD diss., Ball State University, 1967), 119.

3. Ibid., 132.

4. Ibid., 132–33, 143.

5. Ibid., 11.

6. "Abstract of Votes Cast in 1860 for Governor, Lieutenant Governor and State Offices," Indiana Secretary of State, Microfilm Roll Number 6617, Indiana State Archives, Indianapolis, IN.

7. Ibid.

8. "Abstract of Votes Cast for Representative in Congress for 1860 by Congressional District," Indiana State Archives.

9. Wood Gray, *The Hidden Civil War: The Story of the Copperheads* (New York: Viking Press, 1942), 240.

10. Jesse Bright, "Some Letters of Jesse Bright to William H. English, (1842–1863)," *Indiana Magazine of History* 30 (September 1934): 370.

11. E. Duane Elbert, "Southern Indiana in the Election of 1860: The Leadership and the Electorate," *Indiana Magazine of History* 70 (March 1974): 13.

12. Walter Dean Burnham, *Presidential Ballots, 1836–1892* (Baltimore: Johns Hopkins University Press, 1955), 390–408.

13. Jesse Bright, "Some Letters of Jess Bright to William H. English," *Indiana Magazine of History* 30 (September 1934): 385.

14. William Dudley Foulke, *Life of Oliver P. Morton*, 2 vols. (Indianapolis: Bowen-Merrill, 1899), 1:93.

15. *Indianapolis Sentinel*, April 11, 1861.

16. Lorna Lutes Sylvester, "Oliver P. Morton and Hoosier Politics during the Civil War" (PhD diss., Indiana University, 1968), 50.

17. Ibid.

18. Thornbrough, *Indiana in the Civil War Era*, 103.

19. Kenneth Stampp, *Indiana Politics during the Civil War* (Indianapolis: Indiana Historical Bureau, 1949), 73.

20. Thornbrough, *Indiana in the Civil War Era*, 117.

21. Hamilton Family Papers, July 26, 1861, L62, Indiana State Library, Indianapolis, IN.

22. Sylvester, "Oliver P. Morton and Hoosier Politics during the Civil War," 65.

23. Arville L. Funk, *Hoosiers in the Civil War* (Chicago: Adams Press, 1967), 50.

24. Benjamin Kimberlin to Jacob R. Kimberlin, May 26, 1862, Kimberlin Family Papers, private collection (hereafter cited as Kimberlin Papers).

25. John D. Barnhart, "The Impact of the Civil War on Indiana," *Indiana Magazine of History* 57 (September 1961): 200.

26. Muster Rolls, Indiana State Archives.

27. *Report of the Adjutant General of the State of Indiana*, 8 vols. (Indianapolis: Samuel M. Douglass, State Printer, 1865–69), 2:612.

28. Muster Rolls.

29. Kenneth Hafendorfer, *Battle of Richmond, Kentucky* (Louisville: KH Press, 2006), 36.

30. Ibid., 141.

31. Ibid., 217.

32. Ibid., 303.

33. Catharine Merrill, *The Soldier of Indiana in the War for the Union*, 2 vols. (Indianapolis: Merrill and Company, 1866), 1:606–9.

34. *A Chronology of Indiana in the Civil War* (Indianapolis: Indiana Civil War Centennial Commission, 1965), 49.

35. Jacob R. Kimberlin to Isaac Jones Kimberlin, July 30, 1862, Kimberlin Papers.

36. Isaac Jones Kimberlin to Jacob R. Kimberlin, August 22, 1862, ibid.

37. Jacob R. Kimberlin to Isaac Jones Kimberlin, September 4, 1862, ibid.

38. Sylvester, "Oliver P. Morton and Hoosier Politics during the Civil War," 130.

39. *Indiana State Sentinel*, September 22, 1862.

40. Frank Klement, *Copperheads in the Middle West* (Chicago, University of Chicago Press, 1960), 1.

41. Mayo Fesler, "Secret Political Societies in the North during the Civil War," *Indiana Magazine of History* 14 (September, 1918): 203.

42. Ibid., 186–87.

43. Ibid., 200.

44. Foulke, *Life of Oliver P. Morton*, 380.

45. *Paoli Eagle*, January 21, 1861.

46. *Brevier Legislative Reports Embracing Short-hand Sketches of the Debates and Journals of the General Assembly of the State of Indiana*, 17 vols. (Indianapolis: Daily Indiana State Sentinel, 1859–88), 4:5–6.

47. Robert N. Scott, *The War of the Rebellion: A Compilation of the Official Records of the Union and Confederate Armies*, series 1 (Washington, DC: Government Printing Office, 1902), 23, pt 2:237.

48. Fesler, "Secret Political Societies in the North during the Civil War," 232.

49. Ibid., 208.

50. *Report of the Judge Advocate General on "The Order of the American Knights," Alias "The Sons of Liberty": A Western Conspiracy in the Aid of Southern Rebellion* (Washington, DC: Chronicle Printers, 1864), 6.

51. Fesler, "Secret Political Societies in the North during the Civil War," 185.

52. Ibid., 186, 189.

53. Ibid., 251.

54. Ibid., 211.

55. Klement, *Copperheads in the Middle West*, 205.

56. Frank Klement, *Lincoln's Critics: The Copperheads of the North* (Shippensburg, PA: White Mane Books, 1999), 231.

57. Klement, *Copperheads in the Middle West*, 89.

58. Klement, *Lincoln's Critics*, 159.

59. Sylvester, "Oliver P. Morton and Hoosier Politics during the Civil War," 151–52.

60. Ibid., 176.

61. Ibid., 268.

62. Stephen E. Towne, *Surveillance and Spies in the Civil War: Exposing Confederate Conspiracies in America's Heartland* (Athens: Ohio University Press, 2015), 6–7.

63. *Madison Daily and Evening Courier*, November 4, 1862.

64. Sylvester, "Oliver P. Morton and Hoosier Politics during the Civil War," 185.

65. Foulke, *Life of Oliver P. Morton*, 198–99.

66. Ibid., 255.

67. Charles Carlton, *Charles I: The Personal Monarch* (London: Routledge, 1995), 354.

68. *Madison Daily and Evening Courier*, February 24, 1863.

69. March 19, 1863, Sarah Waldschmidt Young Bovard Diary, Scott County Historical Society, Scottsburg, IN.

70. April 14, 1863, ibid.

71. April 22, 1863, ibid.

72. October 4, 1863, ibid.

73. November 25, 1863, ibid.

74. James A. Adams to Catherine Allison, May 17, 1864, James A. Adams Civil War Letters, 1862–1865, William Henry Smith Memorial Library, Indiana Historical Society.

75. Mollie McPheeters to John McPheeters, June 15, 1863, John S. McPheeters Correspondence and Records, 1863–1910, Indiana Historical Society (hereafter cited as McPheeters Correspondence and Records).

76. George McPheeters to Mollie McPheeters, July 1, 1863, ibid.

77. Oliver P. Morton Letters, Indiana Historical Society.

78. Kenneth Stampp, "The Impact of the Civil War upon Hoosier Society," *Indiana Magazine of History* 38 (March 1942): 13.

79. Nora Lewis Dupraz, "A Civil War Story from Vevay," *Indiana Magazine of History* 35 (June, 1939): 158.

80. *Scott County Journal*, September 4, 1924.

81. *Lexington: A Pioneer Town* (Lexington Historical Society), 1988.

82. Vincent Akers, ed., *The Demaree Papers: Letter 1854–1875* (Np., 1970), xi.

83. William Henry Harrison Gookins, "Civil War Letters of Harrison Gookins, a Soldier," *Indiana Writes* 1, no. 3 & 4 (1976): 24.

84. Thornbrough, *Indiana in the Civil War Era*, 138–39.

85. Speech by the Hon. Abraham Lincoln at Chicago, given June 26, 1857, in Response to Mr. Douglas, Chicago, IL, July 10, 1858, in Joseph Fornieri, *The Language of Liberty* (Chicago: Regency, 2004), 218.

86. Henry C. Adams Jr., *Indiana at Vicksburg* (Indianapolis: Indiana-Vicksburg Military Park Commission, 1910), 248

87. Civil War Pension Application Number 965710, Certificate Number 617882, National Archives, Washinton DC.

88. Scott, *War of the Rebellion*, 24, pt. 1:566–67.

89. Kimberlin Papers.

90. Ibid.

91. John S. McPheeters, "A Brief History of the 23rd Regiment of Indiana Volunteers," unpublished manuscript, McPheeters Correspondence and Records.

92. Kimberlin Papers.

93. Ibid.

94. Ibid.

95. John J. Hardin Papers, MS174, L209, Guide to the Indiana Sesquicentennial Manuscript Project: Part 1, Indiana State Library.

96. Scott, *War of the Rebellion*, 24, pt. 1:566–67.

97. Terrence J. Winschel, *Triumph and Defeat: The Vicksburg Campaign* (New York: Savas Publishing, 1999), 143.

98. Ibid., 142.

99. Ibid., 58.

100. Terrence Winschel, interview with the author, Vicksburg National Battlefield Park, March 6, 2006.

101. Adams, *Indiana at Vicksburg*, 249.

102. Winschel, *Triumph and Defeat*, 93.

103. Adams, *Indiana at Vicksburg*, 250.

104. Author reconnaissance of site and Winschel interview.

105. John McPheeters to Mollie McPheeters, McPheeters Correspondence and Records.

106. Kimberlin Papers.

107. Winschel interview.

108. Ibid.

109. McPheeters, "Brief History of the 23rd Regiment of Indiana Volunteers."

110. Kimberlin Papers.

111. Ibid.

112. Thornbrough, *Indiana in the Civil War Era*, 191.

113. Adams, *Indiana at Vicksburg*, 252.

114. Isaac N. Kimberlin to "Brother and Sister," November 3, 1863, Kimberlin Papers.

115. Isaac N. Kimberlin to Jacob R. Kimberlin, December 28, 1863, ibid.

116. John C. Waugh, *Reelecting Lincoln: The Battle for the 1864 Presidency* (New York: Crown Publishers, 1997), 335.

117. Thornbrough, *Indiana in the Civil War Era*, 210.

118. Waugh, *Reelecting Lincoln*, 333.

119. Thornbrough, *Indiana in the Civil War Era*, 220.

120. Isaac N. Kimberlin to Jacob "R.," September 25, 1864, Kimberlin Papers.

121. Waugh, *Reelecting Lincoln*, 335.

122. Calvin Fletcher Diary, November 9, 1864, *The Diary of Calvin Fletcher*, 9 vols. (Indianapolis: Indiana Historical Society, 1972–83), 8:465–68.

123. Adams, *Indiana at Vicksburg*, 253.

124. October 6, 1864, in "Civil War Diary of Robert Armstrong, Sergeant, 66th Indiana Infantry, 1862–1865," typescript, Allen County Public Library, Fort Wayne, IN.

125. John McPheeters to Mollie McPheeters, April 9, 1865, McPheeters Correspondance and Records.

126. May 30, 1865, "Civil War Diary of Robert Armstrong."

Chapter 5

1. Isaac N. Kimberlin to Jacob R., September 25, 1864, private collection (hereaftercited as Kimberlin Papers).

2. Application Number 7130, Certificate Number 9253, Civil War Pension Records, U.S. National Archives, Washington, DC (hereafter cited as NA).

3. Application Number 458371, Certificate Number 279688, Civil War Pension Records, NA.

4. Application Number 965710, Certificate Number 617882, Civil War Pension Records, ibid.

5. Ibid.

6. "Eleventh Missouri Infantry Regimental History," http://civilwararchive.com/ Unreghst/unmoinf3.htm#.

7. Application Number 965710, Certificate Number 617882, Civil War Pension Records, NA.

8. Ibid.

9. Ibid.

10. Ibid.

11. Ibid.

12. Ibid.

13. Ibid.

14. James H. Kimberlin to Jacob R. Kimberlin, March 1, 1864, Kimberlin Papers.

15. Application Number 797901, Certificate Number 559084, Civil War Pension Records, NA.

16. 1880 US Census.

17. 1900 US Census.

18. 1910 US Census.

19. Application #797901, Certificate #559084, Civil War Pension Records, NA.

20. *Report of the Adjutant General of the State of Indiana*, 8 vols. (Indianapolis: Samuel M. Douglass, State Printer, 1865–69), 3:245–47.

21. Jerry O. Porter, *The Sultana Tragedy, America's Greatest Maritime Disaster* (Gretna, LA: Pelican Publishing Company, 2000), 10.

22. Ibid., 12.

23. Ibid., 12–13.

24. Ibid., 20.

25. Typed statement by James. H. Kimberlin in 1918 in an attempt to clarify the events of April 27, 1865, Kimberlin Papers.

26. Ibid.

27. 1880 US Census.

28. Application Number 532120, Certificate Number 315584, Civil War Pension Records, NA.

29. Ibid.

30. Ibid.

31. Ibid.

32. Ibid.

33. 1900 US Census.

34. 1910 US Census.

35. Ibid.

36. Application Number 532120, Certificate Number 315584, Civil War Pension Records, NA.

37. Application Number 797901, Certificate Number 559084, Civil War Pension Records, ibid.

38. Ibid.

39. 1920 US Census.

40. Application Number 532120, Certificate Number 315584, Civil War Pension Records, NA.

41. Ibid.

42. Ibid.

43. Muster Rolls, Indiana State Archives, Indianapolis (hereafter cited as Muster Rolls).

44. 1870 US Census.

45. Application Number 810624, Certificate Number 591599, Civil War Pension Records, NA.

46. 1880 US Census.

47. Civil War Pension Records, Application Number 810624, Certificate Number 591599, NA.

48. Application Number 903605 Certificate Number 681743, NA, ibid.

49. Application Number 810624, Certificate Number 591599, NA, ibid.

50. *Index to Marriage Records: Indiana*, compiled by Works Progress Administration, 1938–1940, Ancstery.com/.

51. Genealogical Research conducted by Denise Moody, Lexington, Kentucky.

52. 1860 US Census.

53. Application Number 755186, Certificate Number 548880, Civil War Pension Records, NA.

54. Muster Rolls.

55. Application Number 755186, Certificate Number 548880, Civil War Pension Records, NA.

56. Ibid.

57. Ibid.

58. Ibid.

59. 1870 US Census.

60. 1880 US Census.

61. 1900 US Census.

62. 1920 US Census.

63. Application Number 755186, Certificate Number 548880, Civil War Pension Records, NA.

64. 1930 US Census, ISL.

65. Application Number 755186, Certificate Number 548880, Civil War Pension Records, NA.

66. Henry C. Adams Jr., *Indiana at Vicksburg* (Indianapolis, Indiana Historical Commission, 1911), 242.

67. Letter from James Stark to Henry Stark, October 17, 1861, Application Number 283073, Certificate Number 200032, Civil War Pension File, NA.

68. Ibid.

69. Affidavit of Henry Stark, Civil War Pension Application Number 283073, Certificate Number 200032, NA.

70. Ibid.

71. Ibid.

72. Ibid.

73. James Stark to Henry Stark, October 17, 1861, Application Number 283073, Certificate Number 200032, Civil War Pension File, NA.

74. Letter from John Schamuel to Commissioner of Pensions, December 31, 1886, Civil War Pension File, ibid.

75. Ibid.

76. Affidavit of Samuel Miller, Application Number 283073, Certificate Number 200032, Civil War Pension File, NA.

77. Affidavit of Mary Rankin and Emeline Fawkes, ibid.

78. Affidavit of Henry Stark, ibid.

79. Ibid.

80. Frank L. Klement, *Lincoln's Critics: The Copperheads of the North* (Shippensburg, PA: White Mane Books, 1999), 149.

81. Indiana Civil War Centennial Commission, *A Chronology of Indiana in the Civil War* (Indianapolis, 1965), 39.

82. Letter from John J. Kimberlin to Jacob R. Kimberlin, April 12, 1863, Kimberlin Papers.

Bibliography

Primary Sources:

Newspapers

Indiana State Sentinel, September 22, 1862.

Indianapolis Sentinel, April 11, 1861.

Lexington Clipper, September 23, 1858.

Madison Courier, April 18, 1854.

Madison Daily and Evening Courier, November 4, 1862, February 24, 1863.

New Albany Weekly Ledger, November, 28, 1860.

Paoli Eagle, January 21, 1861.

Scott County Journal, September 4, 1924.

Manuscript Collections

James Adams Papers. William Henry Smith Memorial Library, Indiana Historical Society.

Robert Armstrong Diary, MS70, L209. Indiana State Library.

Calvin Fletcher Diary. William Henry Smith Memorial Library, Indiana Historical Society.

John J. Hardin Papers, MS174, Collection L209, Indiana State Library.

Kimberlin Family Papers. In Private Hands.

John McPheeters Letters. William Henry Smith Memorial Library, Indiana Historical Society.

Government Documents

Abstract of Votes, Secretary of State Election Returns. Microfilm Roll #6617, Indiana State Archives.

Brevier Legislative Reports, 1861. Vol. I4.

Civil War Pension Files. National Archives. Washington, DC.

Declaration of Soldier for Pension, War of 1812. Record Group 15A-SO 10690. National Archives. Washington, DC.

Index to Marriage Records: Indiana. Compiled by Works Progress Administration, 1938–1940.

Memorial to Congress by Citizens of Clark County. HF: 12 Cong., 2sess: DS, October 15, 1812.

Minute Book, Clark's Grant Board of Commissioners. William Henry Smith Memorial Library, Indiana Historical Society.

Muster Rolls of Indiana Civil War Volunteers. Indiana State Archives.

Report of the Adjutant General of the State of Indiana. Volume 3, *1861–1865*. Indianapolis: Samuel M. Douglass, State Printer, 1866.

Report of the Judge Advocate General on "The Order of the American Knights," Alias "The Sons of Liberty": A Western Conspiracy in the Aid of Southern Rebellion. Washington, DC: Chronicle Printers, 1864.

Scott County Order Book B2, 1823–1826. Scott County Historical Society.

Scott County Order Book Number 1, 1820–1823. First Circuit Court, 1820 November

Term, First Day. Scott County Historical Society.

"Speech by the Hon. Abraham Lincoln at Chicago, in Response to Mr. Douglas, Chicago, IL, July 10, 1858." In *The Language of Liberty*. Edited by Joseph Fornieri. Chicago: Regency, 2004.

State Election Returns, 50-Q, boxes 20–22. Indiana State Archives.

Secondary Sources:

Books

Adams, Jr., Henry C. *Indiana at Vicksburg.* Indianapolis: Indiana–Vicksburg Military Park Commission, 1910.

Barnhart, John Donald. *The Impact of the Civil War on Indiana.* Indianapolis: Indiana Civil War Centennial Commission, 1962.

Bogardus, Carl. *The Centennial History of Austin, Scott County, Indiana.* Paoli, IN: Historical Committee of the Centennial Celebration, 1953.

———. *Early History of Scott County, 1820–1870.* Scottsburg, IN: Scott County Historical Society, 1970.

———. *Pioneer Life in Scott County, Indiana.* Austin, IN: Muscatatuck Press, 1957.

Burnham, Walter Dean. *Presidential Ballots, 1836–1892.* Baltimore: Johns Hopkins University Press, 1955.

Carlton, Charles. *Charles I: The Personal Monarch.* London: Routledge, 1995.

Coleman, Lizzie D. *History of the Pigeon Roost Massacre.* Mitchell, IN: Commercial Print, 1904.

Dunn, Jacob Piatt. *Indiana and Indianans.* 5 vols. Chicago: American Historical Society, 1919.

Esarey, Logan, ed. "Gibson's Message to Colonel Hargrove." In *Messages and Letters of William Henry Harrison.* Indianapolis: Indiana Historical Commission, 1922.

Foulke, William Dudley. *Life of Oliver P. Morton.* 2 vols. Indianapolis: Bowen-Merrill, 1899.

Funk, Arville. *Hoosiers in the Civil War.* Chicago: Adams Press, 1967.

Letters of Harrison Gookins, *Indiana Writes*. Bloomington: Indiana University Press, 1976.

Gray, Wood. *The Hidden Civil War: The Story of the Copperheads*. New York: VikingPress, 1942.

Handfieled, Jr., Gerald F. "Life of William English. In *Gentlemen from Indiana: National Party Candidates, 1836–1940*. Edited by Ralph Gray. Indianapolis: Indiana Historical Bureau, 1977.

Indiana Civil War Centennial Commission. *A Chronology of Indiana in the Civil War, 1861–1865*. Indianapolis: Indiana Civil War centennial Commission, 1965.

Hafendorfer, Kenneth. *Battle of Richmond, Kentucky, August 30, 1862*. Louisville: KH Press, 2006.

Keyser, Charles. *The Life of William H. English*. Philadelphia, Ferguson Brothers, 1880.

Klein, Philip. *President James Buchannan*. University Park: Pennsylvania State University Press, 1962.

Klement, Frank. *The Copperheads in the Middle West*. Chicago: University of Chicago Press, 1960.

———. *Lincoln's Critics: The Copperheads of the North*. Shippensburg, PA: White Mane Books, 1999.

Long, John, ed. *Atlas of Historical County Boundaries*. New York: Charles Scribner and Sons, 1996.

Madison, James H. *The Indiana Way: A State History*. Bloomington: Indiana University Press; Indianapolis: Indiana Historical Society, 1986.

Merrill, Catharine. *The Soldier of Indiana in the War for the Union*. 2 vols. Indianapolis: Merrill and Company, 1866.

Potter, Jerry O. *The Sultana Tragedy: America's Greatest Maritime Disaster*. Gretna, LA: Pelican Publishing Company, 2000.

Riker, Dorothy, and Gayle Thornbrough, eds. *Indiana Election Returns, 1816–1851*. Indianapolis: Indiana Historical Bureau, 1960.

Scott, Robert N. *The War of the Rebellion: A Compilation of the Official Records of the Union and Confederate Armies*. Washington, DC, Government Printing Office, 1902.

Stampp, Kenneth. *America in 1857: A Nation on the Brink*. New York: Oxford University Press, 1990.

———. *Indiana Politics during the Civil War*. Indianapolis, Indiana: Historical Bureau, 1949.

Thornbrough, Emma Lou. *Indiana in the Civil War Era, 1850–1880*. 1965. Reprint, Indianapolis: Indiana Historical Society, 1989.

Thorndale, William, and William Dollarhide. *Map Guide to the U.S. Federal Censuses, 1790–1920*. Baltimore: Genealogical Publishing Company, 1987.

Towne, Stephen E. *Surveillance and Spies in the Civil War: Exposing Confederate Conspiracies in America's Heartland*. Athens: Ohio University Press, 2015.

Walsh, Justin E. *Centennial History of the Indiana General Assembly, 1816–1978.* Indianapolis: Select Committee on the Centennial History of the Indiana General Assembly, 1987.

Waugh, John C. *Reelecting Lincoln: The Battle for the 1864 Presidency.* New York: Crown Publishers, 1997.

Winschel, Terrence J. *Triumph and Defeat: The Vicksburg Campaign.* New York, Savas Publishing, 1999.

Periodicals

Author Unknown. "A Civil War Story from Vevay," *Indiana Magazine of History* 35 (June 1939): 158.

Barnhart, John D. "The Impact of the Civil War on Indiana." *Indiana Magazine of History*, 57 September, 1961.

Brand, Carl Fremont. "The History of the Know Nothing Party in Indiana." *Indiana Magazine of History* 18 (March 1922): 177–206.

Bright, Jesse. "Some Letters of Jesse Bright to William H. English, (1842–1863)." *Indiana Magazine of History* 30 (September 1934): 370–92.

Eidson, William G. With Vincent Akers. "Democratic Attitudes in Johnson County during the Civil War: A Look at the Demaree Papers." *Indiana Magazine of History* 70 (March 1974): 44–69.

Elbert, E. Duane. "Southern Indiana in the Election of 1860: The Leadership and the Electorate." *Indiana Magazine of History* 70 (March 1974): 1–23.

Esarey, Logan. "Pioneer Politics in Indiana." *Indiana Magazine of History* 13 (June 1917): 99–128.

Fesler, Mayo. "Secret Political Societies in the North during the Civil War." *Indiana Magazine of History* 14 (September 1918): 183–286.

Stampp, Kenneth M. "The Impact of the Civil War upon Hoosier Society." *Indiana Magazine of History* 38 (March 1942): 1–16.

Van Bolt, Roger H. "The Rise of the Republican Party in Indiana, 1855–1856." *Indiana Magazine of History* 51 (September 1955): 185–220.

Dissertations

Crane, Philip. "A Political History of Joseph Wright." Ph.D. diss., Indiana University, 1961.

Kelso, Thomas J. "The German-American Vote in the Election of 1860: The Case of Indiana with Supporting Data from Ohio." PhD diss., Ball State University, 1967.

Perry, Marjorie. "Opposition to the Civil War in Indiana." PhD diss., University of Washington, 1931.

Sylvester, Lorna Lutes. "Oliver P. Morton and Hoosier Politics during the Civil War." PhD diss., Indiana University, 1968.

Unpublished Manuscripts

Sarah Waldschmidt Young Bovard Diary. Scott County Historical Society.

Crim, Ruth. "History of the Kimberlin Family of Virginia, Kentucky, and Indiana."

Lexington: A Pioneer Town. Scottsburg, IN, Lexington Historical Society, 1988.

Henretty, Maggie. "A History of Scott County." Typed manuscript. Indiana State Library.

McPheeters, John S. "A Brief History of the 23rd Regiment of Indiana Volunteers." Unpublished manuscript. William Henry Smith Memorial Library, Indiana Historical Society.

Wilson, Mary. With Ann Asher. *Lexington*. Pamphlet. William Henry Smith Memorial Library, Indiana Historical Society.

Appendices

A: Soldiers Alphabetically

Last	First	Units
Hough	Alexander	31st IN Co. D
Hough	Milton T.	66th IN Co. K Co. C, 54th IN
Hough	Samuel K.	4th IN Cav Co. D, 77th IN Co. D
Hough	William A.	66th IN Co. K
Kimberlin	Abraham	66th IN Co. K
Kimberlin	Abraham (Abram)	13th IN Cav Co. E, 38th IN Co. D
Kimberlin	Benjamin F.	23rd IN Co. I
Kimberlin	Daniel F.	66th IN Co. K
Kimberlin	Francie "Marion"	42nd IN Co. K
Kimberlin	George	21st IN Co. D 1st IN Heavy Arty, Co. D
Kimberlin	Henry	49th IN Co. D
Kimberlin	Isaac N.	7th MO Co. G, 11 MO Co.G
Kimberlin	Jacob R.	54th IN Co. E
Kimberlin	Jacob T.	23rd IN Co. I
Kimberlin	James H.	50th IN Co. D 52nd IN, Co. D 137th IN, Co. K
Kimberlin	James Harvey	124th IN Co. E (D)
Kimberlin	John G.	2nd US Vol. Cav Homeguards
Kimberlin	John J.	23rd IN Co. I
Kimberlin	William H.	16th IN Co. F
Kimberlin	William H. H.	23rd IN Co. I
Stark	James	23rd IN Co. I
Whitlach	Barnes (Barnett) R. (Reese)	66th IN Co. K
Whitlach	Charles A.	66th IN Co. K
Whitlach	Charles S.	66th IN Co. K, 144th IN Co. H

Status

Dis 6/13/1865

Dis 6/7/1865

Dis 7/22/1865

WIA, 8/30/1862 Richmond, KY, WIA 8/12/1864 Stander, GA, Dis 6/3/1865

Mus Out 6/3/1865

Mus Out 8/22/1865

KIA, 5/12/1863, Raymond, MS

KIA, 8/30/1862, Richmond, KY

Dis 6/18/1865

Dis 1/10/1866

Dis 7/15/1865

Mus Out 3/1/1866

Mus Out 9/16/1862

WIA 6/4/1863, Vicksburg, Died 8/2, New Albany

Dis 9/10/1865

POW, Andersonville, GA, Released April, 1865

WIA returning deserters

KIA 11/4/1863

WIA, 8/30/1862, Richmond, KY & 1/10/1863, Arkansas Post

KIA, May 1, 1863, Thompsons Hill, MS

Died of disease 1/18/1862

Dis 6/3/1865

Died of disease 12/12/1862

Dis 6/5/1865

A: Soldiers Alphabetically (continued)

Last	First	Units
Whitlach	Henry H.	66th IN Co. K (L)
Whitlach	John H.	66th IN Co. K
Whitlach	John K.	66th IN Co. K, 54th IN Co.E
Whitlach	John S.	66th IN Co. K,
Whitlach	John T.	66th IN Co. K,
Williams	George (1)	93rd IN Co. B
Williams	George (2)	93rd IN Co. B
Williams	Josiah	2nd WI Cav Co. F (6th WI Cav)

Status

WIA, Died October 1, 1864, Marietta, GA Hosp.

Dis 6/3/1865

Died September 10, 1864, Atlanta Hosp.

Dis 1/27/1863 on surg cert. of disability

Died of disease 9/10/1864, Atlanta

Dis 5/16/1863 WIA?

Dis 6/10/1865

Unknown

B: Soldiers by Unit

Last	First	Units
Kimberlin	James Harvey	124th IN Co. E (D)
Hough	Samuel K.	4th IN Co. D, 77th IN Co. D
Kimberlin	Abraham (Abram)	13th IN Cav Co. E, 38th IN Co. D
Kimberlin	William H.	16th IN Co. F
Kimberlin	George	21st IN Co. D, 1st IN Heavy Arty, Co. D
Stark	James	23rd IN Co. I
Kimberlin	Jacob T.	23rd IN Co. I
Kimberlin	Benjamin F.	23rd IN Co. I
Kimberlin	William H. H.	23rd IN Co. I
Kimberlin	John J.	23rd IN Co. I
Kimberlin	John G.	2nd US Vol. Cav Homeguards
Williams	Josiah	2nd WI Cav Co. F (6th WI Cav)
Hough	Alexander	31st IN Co. D
Kimberlin	Francie "Marion"	42nd IN Co. K
Kimberlin	Henry	49th IN Co. D
Kimberlin	James H.	50th IN Co. D, 52nd IN Co. D, 137th IN Co. K
Kimberlin	Jacob R.	54th IN Co. E
Whitlach	John H.	66th IN Co. K
Whitlach	John K.	66th IN Co. K, 54th IN Co. E
Kimberlin	Daniel F.	66th IN Co. K
Hough	William A.	66th IN Co. K
Kimberlin	Abraham	66th IN Co. K
Whitlach	Barnes R. (Reese)	66th IN Co. K
Whitlach	Charles A.	66th IN Co. K
Whitlach	Henry H.	66th IN Co. K (L)
Hough	Milton T.	66th IN Co. K, 54th IN Co. C

Last	First	Units
Whitlach	John S.	66th IN Co. K
Whitlach	John T.	66th IN Co. K
Whitlach	Charles S.	66th IN Co. K, 144th IN Co. H
Kimberlin	Isaac N.	7th MO Co. G, 11th MO, Co. G
Williams	George (1)	93rd IN Co. B
Williams	George (2)	93rd IN Co. B

C: Soldiers by Surname

Last	First	Father	Mother
Hough	Alexander	Able Hough	Anna
Hough	Samuel K.	Alfred Hough	Rebecca Hough
Whitlach	John H.	Barnett K. Whitlach	Angeline Whitlach
Whitlach	John K.	Barnett K. Whitlach	Angeline Whitlach
Whitlach	Barnes R. (Reese)	Charles Kimberlin Whitlach	Sarah "Sallie" Williams
Whitlach	Charles A.	Charles Kimberlin Whitlach	Sarah "Sallie" Williams
Whitlach	John T.	Charles Kimberlin Whitlach	Sarah "Sallie" Williams
Williams	Josiah	Daniel Williams	Mary "Polly" Kimberlin
Hough	Milton T.	Emsley Hough	Belinda Kimberlin
Hough	William A.	Emsley Hough	Belinda Kimberlin
Kimberlin	Francie "Marion"	Fountain Kimberlin	Elizabeth Kinkle
Williams	George (2)	Hazekiah Williams	
Stark	James	Henry Arnold Starkes	Louis Jane Akers
Kimberlin	George	Henry Kimberlin	Mary
Kimberlin	Benjamin F.	Isaac Jones Kimberlin	Christiana Starkes
Kimberlin	Jacob R.	Isaac Jones Kimberlin	Christiana Starkes
Kimberlin	William H. H.	Isaac Jones Kimberlin	Christiana Starkes
Kimberlin	John J.	Jacob J. Kimberlin	Elizabeth Oldham
Kimberlin	Daniel F.	Jacob J. Kimberlin	Elizabeth Oldham
Kimberlin	Isaac N.	Jacob J. Kimberlin	Elizabeth Oldham
Kimberlin	Jacob T.	Jacob J. Kimberlin	Elizabeth Oldham
Kimberlin	William H.	Jacob L. Kimberlin	Nancy Butler
Kimberlin	Abraham	James Washington Kimberlin	Pemalia "Millie" Smith
Kimberlin	Henry	James Washington Kimberlin	Pemalia "Millie" Smith
Kimberlin	James H.	John N. B. "Ponar" Kimberlin	Margaret Dailey
Whitlach	Charles S.	John Whitlach	Jane Smith

Last	First	Father	Mother
Whitlach	Henry H.	John Whitlach	Jane Smith
Williams	George (1)	John Williams	Susannah Kimberlin
Kimberlin	John G.	Joseph Kimberlin	Susan Kimberlin
Kimberlin	James Harvey	Lewis Kimberlin	Olive
Kimberlin	Abraham (Abram)	William H. H. Kimberlin	Elizabeth Betsy Kimberlin
Whitlach	John S.	William Whitlach	Elizabeth "Betsy" Kimberlin

D: Soldiers by Status

Last	First	Status
Stark	James	Died of disease 1/18/1862
Whitlach	Charles A.	Died of disease 12/12/1862
Whitlach	John T.	Died of disease 9/10/1864 Atlanta
Whitlach	John K.	Died September 10, 1864, Atlanta Hosp.
Kimberlin	George	Dis 1/10/1866
Whitlach	John S.	Dis 1/27/1863 on surg cert. of disability
Williams	George (1)	Dis 5/16/1863 WIA?
Williams	George (2)	Dis 6/10/1865
Hough	Alexander	Dis 6/13/1865
Kimberlin	Francie "Marion"	Dis 6/18/1865
Whitlach	Barnes R. (Reese)	Dis 6/3/1865
Whitlach	John H.	Dis 6/3/1865
Whitlach	Charles S.	Dis 6/5/1865
Hough	Milton T.	Dis 6/7/1865
Kimberlin	Henry	Dis 7/15/1865
Hough	Samuel K.	Dis 7/22/1865
Kimberlin	James H.	Dis 9/10/1865
Kimberlin	John J.	KIA 11/4/1863
Kimberlin	Benjamin F.	KIA, 5/12/1863, Raymond, MS
Kimberlin	Daniel F.	KIA, 8/30/1862, Richmond, KY
Kimberlin	William H. H.	KIA, May 1, 1863, Thompsons Hill, MS
Whitlach	Henry H.	WIA, Died October 1, 1864, Marietta, GA Hosp.
Kimberlin	Isaac N.	Mus Out 3/1/1866
Kimberlin	Abraham	Mus Out 6/3/1865
Kimberlin	Abraham (Abram)	Mus Out 8/22/1865
Kimberlin	Jacob R.	Mus Out 9/16/1862

Last	First	Status
Kimberlin	James Harvey	POW, Andersonville, GA, Released April, 1865
Kimberlin	Jacob T.	WIA 6/4/1863, Vicksburg, Died, 8/2, New Albany
Kimberlin	John G.	WIA returning deserters
Hough	William A.	WIA, 8/30/1862 Richmond, KY, WIA 8/12/1864 Stander, GA, Dis 6/3/1865
Kimberlin	William H.	WIA, 8/30/1862, Richmond, KY & 1/10/1863, Arkansas Post
Williams	Josiah	Unknown

Index

Twenty-second Indiana, 90
Twenty-third Indiana, 1, 5, 6, 7, 10, 62,
72, 75, 76, 77, 79, 81–82, 83, 84, 87, 89,
94, 97, 106, 110, 113; (illus.), 78
Tyler, John, 27, 39

Uncle Tom's Cabin, 44
Union Party, 66, 70, 87
United States Commissioner of
Pensions, 111
United States National Archives, 91–92
United States Treasury Department, 27

Vallandigham, Clement, 60, 66, 72
Vallonia, 20
Van Buren, Martin, 37, 38, 39, 40
Van Dorn, Earl, 81, 82
Varble, Daniel, 65
Varble, James, 65
Varble, John, 65
Vernon, 103
Vevay, 72
Vicksburg, battle of, 72, 75, 76, 78, 79,
81, 82, 83–84, 94, 97, 101, 106; (illus.),
76, 77
Vienna, 20, 28, 73, 84
Vincennes, 3, 12, 14, 20
Volusia Silt Loam, 12
Von Bosse, Georg, 56
Voorhees, Daniel, 60–61, 66, 68, 87, 89;
(illus.), 59

Wall, James Walter, 68
Wallace, Lew, 62
War of 1812, pp. 13, 108

War pensions, 92–93, 95, 96, 99, 100, 103,
104–5, 106, 107, 110, 111, 112–13
Ward, James, 13
Washington County, 5
Watson, James, 105
Waverly Silt Loam, 12
Welles, Gideon: (illus.), 66
Western Eagle, 13, 14
Whig Party, 23, 33, 35, 36, 37
Whitcomb, James, 39, 40, 42
White, I. N., 18
White, Joseph, 38
White family, 111
Whitlach, Alexander, 65
Whitlach, Barnett, 44
Whitlach, John S., 65
Whitlach, Reace, 65
Whitlach, Sarah. *See* Gladden, Sarah
Whitlach
Whitlach, William, 108
Whitlach (Whitlatch) family, 4, 23, 34, 65,
87, 112
Wick, William W., 35
Willard, Ashbel, 50, 53
Williams, Absolum, 24
Williams, John, 4
Williams, Nancy Kimberlin, 24
Williams family, 4, 112
Wilson, John, 50
Wirt, William, 36
Wood Township (Clark County), 28
Wright, Joseph, 40, 41, 44, 53

Zollicatter (LA), 109